Luscious
VEGETARIAN

Luscious
VEGETARIAN

Sonia Cabano and Jade de Waal

Photography by Sean Calitz

Published in 2012 by Struik Lifestyle
(an imprint of Random House Struik (Pty) Ltd)
Company Reg. No 1966/003153/07
Wembley Square, Solan Road, Cape Town 8001 South Africa
PO Box 1144 Cape Town 8000 South Africa

www.randomstruik.co.za

ISBN 978-177007-961-8 (Print)
ISBN 978-143230-142-2 (e-Pub)
ISBN 978-143230-143-9 (Pdf)

Publisher: Linda de Villiers
Managing editor: Cecilia Barfield
Design manager: Beverley Dodd
Editors: Browen Leak and Anja Grobler
Designer: Helen Henn
Photographer: Sean Calitz
Stylist: Brita du Plessis
Stylist assistant: Yvette Pascoe
Indexer: Anja Grobler

Reproduction by Resolution
Printing and binding by Times Offset (M) SDN BHD

Contents

Introduction

WHY VEGETARIAN?

There are many reasons to adopt a plant-based diet, be they economic, medical or ethical. Far from being dull and boring, a plant-based diet offers a rich variety of ingredients —which are both nutritious and delicious — with which to nourish our bodies and pleasure our senses.

Nutritionally related diseases like diabetes, cancer and heart disease have become global epidemics. Our bodies are baulking at our poor diets and lifestyles by becoming sick and dysfunctional from ever-younger ages. And with food contamination and even global food scarcity looming on the horizon, the natural vegetarian option is becoming increasingly more attractive if you want to become a more conscientious, ethical consumer. Vegetarianism gently eases you into a more harmonious relationship with yourself and your environment, freeing up your body's detoxification organs and promoting a sense of abundant wellbeing.

More than ever, we need to start making dietary choices that support a sustainable lifestyle that harms neither our bodies nor the environment. High-density animal farming has a devastating impact on the environment, and the animals are often subjected to cruel and inhumane treatment in order to provide us with food. You wouldn't want to cram steroids, antibiotics and hormones into your body from your bathroom cabinet, so why would you want to ingest it via the food you eat? Animals transported and slaughtered in abattoirs under stress, release huge amounts of the stress hormones cortisol and adrenalin, which are directly absorbed into your body when you eat the meat, thus placing massive strain on your own organs too.

We wrote this book out of love — love for food and cooking, love for the environment, and love for natural wellbeing. We hope that *Luscious Vegetarian* can assist and entice you to explore and experiment with recipes that will create a healthier, more ethically sound lifestyle. Recipes have been very carefully chosen for universal appeal, to satisfy the requirements of everyone from young professionals, singletons and athletes, to the health-conscious, hedonists and bustling families alike.

WHY THIS BOOK?

There are many vegetarian cookbooks available to the South African consumer, most of which are imported and therefore not truly reflective of the South African lifestyle. Many also rely on ingredients that may be awkward for local consumers to source. Alternatively, many vegetarian cookbooks propose a lifestyle change or adaptation so daunting that it may seem off-putting to all but the most fervently committed vegetarians.

With this book, we set out to demonstrate that vegetarian cooking need not be synonymous with a dull and spartan dietary regime, but can instead be a celebration of nature's luscious bounty available all year round. Using mostly local, seasonal and, where possible, organic ingredients, the recipes cover the full range from easy, quick everyday dishes, light bites and simple snacks, to rejuvenation and detoxification with pure foods, to hedonistic feasts for celebrations and deeply satisfying soul food, as well as marvellous bakes and sweet treats.

How to cook vegetarian

Many people think of vegetarian food as bland, heavy stodge. 'I never seem to feel full' is another complaint. In fact, plant food correctly prepared and served is beautiful, colourful and extremely tasty.

Getting enough protein shouldn't be a problem provided you make ample use of pulses, grains, nuts, cheese and eggs or soy products. To ensure your happiness at the table, try to think first about how you compose a plate and a meal – include contrasting textures such as crunchy, juicy and smooth or slippery, and serve hot and cold, bland and spicy, and moist and dry foods together.

Low-GI foods such as beans and whole grains keep blood-sugar levels stable for longer, which means no sudden awkward hunger pangs. But do make sure you don't overdo it with refined starches, sugars and saturated fats, since that will play havoc with your blood-sugar levels, energy and weight. Moderation is still the best advice!

It's not necessary to buy a shelf full of vitamins and supplements. We find that a few tablespoons of unsulphured blackstrap molasses daily provides healthy amounts of potassium, iron and magnesium, and regular vitamin B complex injections will help keep you nourished.

Good basics to have in your pantry

Whipping up tasty treats in a hurry poses no problem at all if you've got a cupboard decently stocked with the basics, and make liberal use of leftovers. Start by doing a little planning ahead for the week's meals. When cooking rice, grains, beans, pasta or potatoes, for example, cook twice the usual amount and chill what is not used. This way you'll always have a handy staple around which to plan a meal. (Just make sure food is thoroughly cool before you refrigerate it; refrigerating warm food is a breeding ground for harmful bacteria such as salmonella which causes food poisoning.)

Take your pick from the following:

Rice – short- and long-grain brown, white basmati, brown basmati, Thai fragrant, risotto, glutinous (for congee), jasmine, brown and wild mix, red, black rice
Grains – dehusked millet, barley, buckwheat (kasha), quinoa, couscous, bulgur wheat, polenta, whole wheat (stampkoring), oats, maize kernels (dried, frozen or canned), rye
Pasta and Asian noodles
Breads, etc. – bread rolls, loaf bread, frozen pastry, wraps, tortillas, frozen pancakes, tacos, waffles, English muffins, pitas, croissants, readymade pizza bases, bagels; bread freezes very well for a couple of weeks
Pulses – dried: red, yellow, brown and Puy lentils; canned: small and large white kidney, red kidney, cannellini, butter and borlotti beans, samp and beans, brown lentils, chickpeas, three-bean mix, baked beans in tomato sauce
Eggs – free-range chicken, quail, duck, goose

Non-animal rennet, soft white and hard yellow cheeses and dairy – milk, yoghurt, cream, crème fraîche, mascarpone, paneer, ricotta, labneh, goat's milk cheese, sheep's milk cheese, vegetarian Parmesan and pecorino; ask your deli or supermarket to source stock for you

Oils and fats – extra-virgin olive oil for salads and seasoning, blended olive oil for cooking, sunflower, peanut and canola oils for cooking, sesame oils for Asian cooking, speciality oils for seasoning, ghee, unsalted dairy butter, canola or olive oil margarine

Basic seasonings – sea-salt flakes, cook's all-purpose salt, sesame salt, herb salt, light, dark and sweet Indonesian soy sauces, white and black peppercorns, ground pepper

Vinegars – rice, sherry, wine and malt vinegars (plain or flavoured), balsamic glaze and vinegar, sake, mirin (a fortified Japanese wine used only for cooking)

Herbs and spices – fresh and dried, garlic, ginger

Asian flavours – miso (fermented concentrated soy paste), tahini (sesame paste), hoisin, vegetarian Asian black bean and chilli pastes

Sugars – honey (preferably single-flower organic, non-pasteurised), organic white and brown sugar, palm sugar, barley malt syrup, rice syrup

Tofu – several kinds are available: soft, silken tofu is like barely set custard, best used for mayonnaises, mousses, sauces; firm tofu has been compressed, and is often sold smoked or spiced, can be cubed, grilled, fried or deep-fried

Flours – gram or besan (chickpea flour), potato, rice and soy flour. All are easily obtainable from health stores or the health section of good supermarkets. If they don't stock it, ask for it!

EQUIPMENT

It's not necessary to invest a fortune in getting your kitchen ready for vegetarian cooking. However, since you'll want to make the most of fresh and natural produce, you're going to be doing more of your own food processing rather than relying on stores and factories to do it for you. Remember always to buy the best you can afford since quality appliances last longer and work better.

SOME ITEMS WE SUGGEST YOU INVEST IN INCLUDE THE FOLLOWING:

- We find a really sturdy, large-capacity food processor and a hand-held stick blender indispensible for the time-consuming tasks of blending, grinding, chopping and liquidising. The whisk attachment of a stick blender will help you to become a master of mayonnaise-making too, and it is ideal for whipping up frothy smoothies and lassis.
- Our most cherished luxury is a centrifugal juice extractor – we simply couldn't live without it.
- An ice-cream maker is highly desirable.
- You will need a sturdy mortar and pestle, or an electric coffee grinder used exclusively for grinding spices. (You wouldn't want to drink masala-flavoured coffee, would you?)
- A selection of good-quality, heavy-bottomed, stainless-steel pots and pans, with tight-fitting lids where necessary, from 500 ml to 6 litre capacity are essentials. Try to have at least one 10 litre-capacity stockpot for stocks and sauces.
- Invest in a large conical sieve for making yoghurt, labneh, etc. and sturdy round large and small sieves for sifting dry ingredients. You will also want muslin or a supply of new J-cloths for straining.
- When it comes to knives, purchase the best you can afford. Don't go for gimmicks as advertised on television. Rather go to a decent kitchen shop and ask for advice. Start with one or two and build a collection, and get them professionally sharpened!

ABOUT SONIA

I grew up very close to nature in a small country village, intensely aware of the seasons and our human dependence on the earth. Like most country folk around us, we thrived on a simple diet of pure and local, seasonal foods. I was immersed from an early age in the typically carnivorous culture of rural South Africa, where meat was practically a staple and often consumed at every meal. Fortunately for us, my mother was a passionate and natural cook and baker, who grew her own vegetables and fresh herbs and kept an orchard with which to augment her cooking. She also took a very keen interest in natural living and wholesome eating. Preservatives, refined sugars and starches as well as adulterated food were anathema to her, with the result that I have always been extremely aware of sound nutrition based on natural, local and seasonal ingredients. For me food is a source of nourishment and pleasure, as well as healing. As a professional cook and food writer, this remains my guiding principle in devising menus and dishes for my clients as well as my own family.

After a health scare a few years ago, I took professional advice and became less reliant on animal sources of protein, which can lead to an over-acidic system and inflammatory diseases. I still eat meat, chicken and fish as well as dairy products occasionally, but choose to use these ingredients more as condiments to supplement a largely plant-based diet. As a very busy working mother of two small children I am acutely aware of the challenges inherent in providing fast, tasty and nutritious meals that do not merely rely on the convenience of animal protein as a main course. Since we are also very active, keeping up energy levels and strength is a constant concern. Trial and error, as well as a lot of research, has aided me in developing recipes that meet with all the above criteria. Since I also believe that eating well is non-negotiable, my recipes create luscious food so good you won't even notice the absence of meat.

ABOUT JADE

I am a keen and creative cook who grew up in a food-loving family, where everyone happily pitches in to prepare the luscious feasts we are famous for, be it breakfast or a no-holds barred dinner party for fifty. When my gold-medal winning athlete younger sister recently converted to a meat-free lifestyle, the entire family rallied behind her and enthusiastically set about experimenting with and exploring deeply satisfying vegetarian recipes.

My dishes demonstrate how to eat consciously without preaching nutrition, by using natural, seasonal produce. My ingredients range from stock available at the corner shop to more lavish and exotic substances such as quinoa, sesame oil and dried olives, which may seem like salt and pepper to more seasoned cooks, but which are unknown to the 'new' converts to vegetarianism. Our recipes will help pave the way for hesitant readers to embrace vegetarian eating, as well as provide some balance for carnivores, seducing the senses while satisfying the appetite.

Simply put, vegetarian eating is kinder to your body, your wallet and the environment. Eating lusciously naturally, is an everyday celebration of being alive. Vegetarian cooking our way bursts with freshness and flavour, is packed with nutrients and can be as hedonistically indulgent as the usual Western diet.

Sonia and Jade

Quick

FROM STOVE TO TABLE IN A FLASH

Sweet couscous with pecans, cranberries and coconut

Use instant wholewheat couscous or bulgur wheat for this refreshing, summery breakfast bowl.

½ cup (125 ml) boiling water
½ cup (125 ml) orange juice
1 T (15 ml) olive oil
2 T (30 ml) icing sugar
¼ t (1 ml) ground cinnamon
grated zest of ½ orange
1 cup (250 ml) instant wholewheat
    couscous or bulgur wheat
2 T (30 ml) pumpkin seeds
2 T (30 ml) roughly chopped pecan nuts
¼ cup (60 ml) dried cranberries or
    chopped dried fruit strips
¼ cup (60 ml) desiccated coconut curls,
    lightly toasted
Greek yoghurt to serve

1. Mix the boiling water, orange juice, olive oil, icing sugar, cinnamon and orange zest together and pour over the couscous or bulgur wheat. Stir well. Cover with a plate and allow to stand for 10–15 minutes before fluffing up with a fork.
2. Scatter over the pumpkin seeds, pecan nuts and dried cranberries or dried fruit strips. Garnish with the toasted coconut curls and serve with dollops of Greek yoghurt on top.

Serves 4

Scrambled eggs with tomato, avocado and rocket

Somehow the textures, flavours and mood of this dish are just drop-dead gorgeous. Eat it with a crusty baguette or toast for optimum delight. The secret to extra-creamy scrambled eggs is to keep the heat very low, stirring constantly and cooking until just set to a creamy curd.

handful of baby Rosa tomatoes or
    1 big ripe tomato
2 large free-range eggs
6 T (90 ml) milk
salt and pepper
1 T (15 ml) butter
1 small ripe avocado, diced or sliced
handful of fresh rocket or basil
fresh crusty bread to serve

1. Cook the tomatoes without oil in a small frying pan for 2 minutes over high heat until bursting. Remove from the pan and set aside. Lower the heat.
2. Whisk the eggs and milk in a jug, and season to taste.
3. Melt the butter in the pan used for the tomatoes and cook the egg mixture over a very gentle heat for 5–7 minutes until creamy and set.
4. Season the avocado and arrange on a plate. Pile the tomatoes, eggs and rocket or basil on top and serve immediately with fresh crusty bread.

Serves 1

TOASTED RAISIN BREAD WITH HONEY FIGS AND RICOTTA

Fresh ricotta is a versatile low-fat, soft, white cheese easily made at home (see page 182).

4 fresh figs, quartered, or 8 dried
    fig halves
4 nectarines, halved (optional)
3–4 T (45–60 ml) organic honey, warmed
200–250 g fresh ricotta
4 slices raisin bread, toasted
    and buttered
2 T (30 ml) pine kernels, toasted (you can
    use pecans or pistachios instead)

1. Preheat the oven's grill.
2. If using dried fig halves, briefly rehydrate by soaking them in warm water for 15 minutes and draining well.
3. Place the fruit, cut-side up, on a baking tray and brush lightly with the warmed honey. Grill for 10 minutes until softened and very lightly charred in spots.
4. Spread ricotta over the buttered toast, arrange the grilled fruit and pine kernels on top, drizzle with some more honey and serve.

COOK'S TIP: Toast the pine kernels in a dry frying pan over medium heat – keep watching as they scorch easily.

Serves 4

SPICED BANANA AND CHOC-CHIP MUFFINS

Overripe bananas are perfect for baking or smoothies – in this super-easy recipe they lend a sweet moistness. The muffins will be good for a day or two. They take just a few minutes to mix and 15 minutes to bake.

2 cups (500 ml) cake flour
pinch of ground nutmeg
1/2 t (2.5 ml) ground cinnamon
2 t (10 ml) baking powder
5 T (75 ml) soft brown sugar
3 overripe bananas, chopped or mashed
    with a fork
1/2 cup (125 ml) chocolate or carob chips
1/3 cup (80 ml) sunflower oil
1 cup (250 ml) soy milk or buttermilk
1 egg

1. Preheat the oven to 180 °C. Spray and line a 12-hole muffin tray with muffin paper cups.
2. Mix the dry ingredients with the banana and chocolate or carob chips in a large bowl, stirring until just combined. The batter must be lumpy.
3. Whisk the oil, milk and egg together until smooth and stir into the banana mixture. Stir until just combined – overworking the batter will make the muffins dense. A few patches of dry flour here and there will do no harm.
4. Spoon the batter into the muffin tray and bake for 15–18 minutes until a toothpick inserted into the centre of a muffin comes out clean. Allow to cool for 10 minutes before serving.

Makes 12

TOMATO SWEETCORN SOUP WITH NACHOS, CHEDDAR AND JALAPEÑOS

Simple, tasty and filling, this is a soupy version of cheesy baked nachos. Peel fresh tomatoes by covering them with boiling water for 2 minutes, after which the skins will slip off easily. Vegans, leave out the cheese.

1 large onion, peeled and finely chopped
2 T (30 ml) olive oil
½ t (2.5 ml) crushed fresh garlic
1 x 410 g can chopped peeled tomatoes
3 medium, ripe red tomatoes, peeled
    and chopped
½ t (2.5 ml) dried origanum
2 cups (500 ml) strong vegetable stock
½ cup (125 ml) sweetcorn (creamed
    or kernel)
salt and pepper, and sugar
2 T (30 ml) sliced pickled jalapeño
    chillies (substitute with
      1 T (15 ml) chopped fresh green chilli
      and 1 t (5 ml) red wine vinegar)
about 24 nachos, any flavour
1 cup (250 ml) grated strong
    Cheddar cheese
chopped fresh coriander to serve

1. Cook the onion in the olive oil in a large saucepan over medium heat until translucent. Add the garlic and cook for another 2 minutes without browning.
2. Add the canned and fresh tomatoes, origanum and stock and simmer for about 20 minutes until nicely aromatic.
3. Crush the tomatoes with a potato masher, or use a hand-held blender.
4. Stir in the sweetcorn and cook for a further 5–7 minutes until heated through. Taste for seasoning and correct with a little sugar if too tart.
5. Ladle into soup bowls. Garnish with a few slices of jalapeño, some crushed nachos and grated cheese. Sprinkle over coriander and serve. Eat carefully – hot, melted cheese can burn your chin and mouth!

Serves 4

MOROCCAN EGGS

A firm favourite with my family – my dad swears these Moroccan eggs will kill any hunger and cure any hangover. - Jade

2 sweet peppers, green and yellow,
    deseeded and sliced 1 cm thick
2 onions, peeled and chopped
1–2 t (5–10 ml) crushed fresh garlic
1 fresh chilli, deseeded and
    finely chopped
1 t (5 ml) ground cumin
olive oil for frying
4 large eggs
salt and pepper
handful of fresh flat-leaf parsley, chopped

1. Cook the peppers, onions, garlic, chilli and cumin in a little olive oil in a frying pan over medium heat until softened but not brown.
2. Use the back of a wooden spoon to make four hollows in the sauce. Drizzle a little olive oil before cracking an egg into each hollow. Turn the heat to low.
3. Put a lid or plate over the pan and continue to cook until the eggs are done to your liking — just set, or firm.
4. Season to taste, scatter over some parsley and serve straight from the pan with hot buttered toast.

Serves 4

CRISPY SPAGHETTI, HERB AND PARMESAN OMELETTE

Don't throw away leftover cooked pasta. Fried until crispy and cooked into a frittata or thin omelette, last night's pasta becomes today's tasty lunch or supper.

6 large eggs
3 T (45 ml) grated Parmesan
4 sundried tomato halves, chopped
2 T (30 ml) chopped fresh herbs (basil,
    parsley, dill, chives, etc.)
salt and pepper
¼ cup (60 ml) butter or oil
2 handfuls of cooked spaghetti (about
    30 g dry uncooked per person)

1. Beat the eggs with the Parmesan, sundried tomatoes, herbs and seasoning.
2. Heat half of the butter or oil in a small non-stick omelette pan and fry half of the cooked spaghetti until crispy.
3. Pour over half of the egg mixture and cook until barely set. Fold in half and slide onto a plate. Keep warm while cooking the second omelette.

Serves 2

SPICY POTATO ROTIS WITH FRESH CORIANDER CHUTNEY

A popular Indian snack turns into a filling meal wrapped in a warm roti. Make the chutney with a hand-held stick blender or food processor and add some chopped onion and tomato relish too. Use cold cooked potatoes.

¼ cup (60 ml) sunflower oil
1 T (15 ml) black mustard seeds
2 t (10 ml) crushed fresh garlic
2 t (10 ml) cayenne pepper or chilli flakes
1 T (15 ml) fennel seeds
1 t (5 ml) each of crushed coriander,
    cumin and sesame seeds
¼ t (1 ml) ground turmeric
2 t (10 ml) grated fresh ginger
500 g potatoes, boiled whole in the skin
    until just tender, peeled and cut into
    2 cm cubes
salt and pepper
4 rotis

1. Heat the oil in a large frying pan with a tight-fitting lid. Add the mustard seeds and cook until they just start to pop.
2. Quickly add the garlic, cayenne pepper or chilli flakes, fennel seeds, turmeric and ginger, and cook over high heat while stirring constantly for about 5 minutes.
3. Add the diced cooked potato and toss in the aromatic spices for about 10 minutes until crispy and golden brown on all sides. Season to taste and drain on absorbent paper towel.
4. Serve hot, wrapped in rotis with atchar or the following coriander chutney.

Serves 4

FRESH CORIANDER CHUTNEY

The easiest is to pop everything into your food processor and blend until fine, but chopping by hand gives a good result.

1 small onion, peeled and very
    finely chopped
½ t (2.5 ml) each of crushed fresh garlic,
    grated fresh ginger, ground cumin,
    sugar and salt
3 T (45 ml) lemon juice
¼ cup (60 ml) Bulgarian yoghurt
50 g fresh coriander leaves,
    finely chopped
large handful of fresh mint leaves,
    stripped off stems and very
    finely chopped

1. Combine all the ingredients and allow to stand for 20 minutes for the flavours to develop.

Makes roughly 1 cup (250 ml)

FAST SUMMER MINESTRONE WITH PESTO

1 stalk celery, chopped
2 large carrots, peeled and chopped
1 leek (white part only), chopped and
    rinsed thoroughly
3 T (45 ml) olive oil
1 large potato, peeled and chopped
3 cups (750 ml) vegetable stock
2 tomatoes, chopped
½ cup (125 ml) macaroni or
    pasta shapes
1 x 400 g can four-bean mix, drained
    and rinsed
handful of fine green beans, topped,
    tailed and chopped
2 courgettes, sliced
¼ cup (60 ml) basil or any other pesto
fresh crusty bread to serve

1. Cook the celery, carrots and leek in the olive oil in a pot
   for 5–6 minutes.
2. Add the remaining ingredients, except the pesto, and
   simmer for 20–30 minutes until the vegetables and
   pasta are tender.
3. Serve with dollops of pesto and some fresh crusty
   bread alongside.

Serves 4

10-MINUTE SUMMER BEAN SALAD WITH NUT-CRUSTED HALLOUMI

1 x 400 g can four-bean mix
1 cup (250 ml) sweetcorn kernels
1 cup (250 ml) cherry tomatoes, halved
3 stalks celery, very finely chopped
1 small onion or 6 spring onions,
    finely chopped
2 t (10 ml) dried tarragon
1 t (5 ml) dried dill
½ cup (125 ml) Bulgarian yoghurt
juice of 1 lemon
salt and pepper
250 g halloumi, cut in 1 cm-thick slices
2 T (30 ml) pine kernels
olive oil for frying
fresh crusty bread to serve

1. Combine all the ingredients except the halloumi, pine
   kernels and oil in an attractive serving bowl. Season well
   and set aside for the flavours to marry.
2. Meanwhile, press each slice of halloumi firmly into some
   pine kernels and fry for 20–30 seconds each side in hot
   olive oil until just golden brown. Serve immediately with the
   summer bean salad and nice crusty bread.

Serves 2-4

30-MINUTE BEAN SOUP WITH CHEESY TOASTS

Proper old-fashioned bean soup, good as it is, takes an age to cook. Using canned beans gets this version from stove to table in just over 30 minutes. This is a real rib-sticker for winter. Vegans omit the cheese and spread the toasties with black olive tapenade.

1 large onion, peeled and very
    finely chopped
2 T (30 ml) olive oil
1 t (5 ml) crushed fresh garlic
1 medium carrot, peeled and finely grated
1 large tomato, grated
1 stalk celery, grated
6 mushrooms, very finely chopped
few sprigs fresh thyme, chopped
2 x 410 g cans beans (sugar or borlotti
    beans work very well)
4 cups (1 litre) strong vegetable or
    mushroom stock
2 T (30 ml) tomato concentrate
1 T (15 ml) blackstrap molasses
    or Marmite
8 slices French bread, lightly toasted
1 cup (250 ml) grated Gruyère or
    mature Cheddar cheese or
    4 T (60 ml) black olive tapenade
salt and pepper
fruity extra-virgin olive oil to serve

1. Cook the onion in the olive oil in a large, heavy-bottomed pot over medium heat until soft and translucent. Add the garlic and cook for a further 2 minutes.
2. Add all the vegetables and the thyme, stir very well and put on the lid for 5–7 minutes. This 'sweats' and softens the vegetables faster.
3. Add the beans in their liquid, the stock, tomato concentrate and molasses or Marmite. Stir well, put on the lid and cook on high for 15 minutes, stirring now and then.
4. In the meantime, make the toasties. Top each slice of toast with cheese and grill until brown and melted. Alternatively brush with olive oil and spread with tapenade if vegan, set aside until needed.
5. Remove the pot from the stove and liquidise the soup with a stick blender, potato masher or food processor.
6. Season to taste and serve topped with the cheese or tapenade toasties. Drizzle over some fruity extra-virgin olive oil at the table.

Serves 4

SWEETCORN, BEAN AND JALAPEÑO QUESADILLAS

Use tortillas that have gone slightly stale for this quick snack - give your creativity free rein when it comes to fillings. Canned samp and beans or drained, rinsed canned beans provide protein.

1 cup (500 ml) frozen sweetcorn, thawed

1 cup (250 ml) canned beans, rinsed and drained

½ cup (125 ml) peeled and very thinly sliced red onion

¼ cup (60 ml) sliced pickled jalapeños, or to taste

2 cups (500 ml) grated cheese (any kind will do)

2 T (30 ml) chopped fresh coriander

8 large tortillas

1. Combine all the ingredients in a mixing bowl.
2. Divide the filling evenly between four tortillas, spreading it out to cover the entire base.
3. Top each with another tortilla and cook one at a time in a large frying pan over medium heat for about 5 minutes on each side. Cut into wedges and serve warm.

Serves 4

INDONESIAN PEANUT DIP

This is addictive as a dip for crunchy vegetable sticks and breadsticks, or even as a dressing for cooked noodles with lightly cooked vegetables and bean sprouts. Roasted sweet potato wedges or chargrilled aubergine (eggplant) slices make champion companions.

2 T (30 ml) peanut oil

1 small onion, peeled and finely minced

2 t (10 ml) crushed fresh garlic

2 t (10 ml) chilli flakes or chopped and deseeded fresh chilli

1 T (15 ml) soft brown sugar

¼ cup (60 ml) light soy sauce

2 T (30 ml) lime juice

½ t (2.5 ml) salt

½ t (2.5 ml) pepper

1 x 400 g jar crunchy peanut butter

2 x 400 ml cans low-fat coconut milk

1. Heat the oil in a frying pan and fry the onion, garlic and chilli over medium heat until the onion is soft and translucent.
2. Add the sugar, soy sauce, lime juice, salt, pepper and peanut butter, and stir until smooth.
3. Cook for about 2 minutes before adding the coconut milk, whisking hard until smooth.
4. Turn down the heat to low and simmer until thickened. Remove from the heat and leave to cool completely before storing in an airtight container in the fridge for up to 1 month.

Makes about 2 cups (500 ml)

PARMESAN-CRUSTED RATATOUILLE WITH MILLET

Oven-baked ratatouille is such a breeze to make and tastier than canned, so do give this recipe a bash. Dehusked millet is an easy-to-cook, high-protein grain. You can use quinoa or dehusked buckwheat (kasha) instead. Toast the grains in some hot oil or ghee for a minute or two before adding stock or water to the pot. This gives it a nuttier taste and removes astringency.

350 g courgettes, washed and chopped
    into 3 cm chunks
2 large aubergines (eggplants), washed
    and cut into 3 cm squares
4 large sweet peppers, washed, deseeded
    and cut into 4 cm squares
2 T (30 ml) extra-virgin olive oil
1 T (15 ml) crushed fresh garlic
2 t (10 ml) chopped fresh rosemary
1 t (5 ml) dried thyme or ½ t (2.5 ml)
    chopped fresh
salt and pepper
1 x 400 g can chopped tomatoes
1 T (15 ml) balsamic vinegar
2 T (30 ml) slivered almonds or
    pine kernels
½ cup (125 ml) grated Parmesan

MILLET
2 T (30 ml) oil
1 cup (250 ml) dehusked millet,
    thoroughly rinsed
1 t (5 ml) crushed fresh garlic
2 cups (500 ml) hot water or
    vegetable stock
salt and pepper

1. Preheat the oven to 200 °C and spread the courgettes, aubergines and peppers in a single layer in a baking dish.
2. Mix the olive oil with the garlic, herbs, salt and pepper, and pour over the vegetables. Stir well to combine thoroughly.
3. Roast in the oven for about 30 minutes until tender and slightly browned.
4. Remove from the oven and pour over the tomatoes and balsamic vinegar. Stir very well again and sprinkle over the almonds or pine kernels and Parmesan. Bake for a further 15 minutes until a crust has formed on top of the ratatouille.
5. To make the millet, heat the oil in a large saucepan and fry the millet and garlic for about 2 minutes until nutty and aromatic. Add the water or stock, season and simmer for about 15 minutes until tender. Spoon onto plates, top with the ratatouille, and sprinkle over extra Parmesan and nuts before serving immediately.

COOK'S TIPS: Ratatouille is great on pasta or mash. Use well-reduced ratatouille as a filling for a pie with a flaky pastry top (see rough puff pastry on page 172).
Cooked, cooled millet mixed with mashed beans makes great vegetarian burgers — just season and form into patties, and chill for 30 minutes before frying or baking.

Serves 4

Chunky bean, tomato, butternut and rice bowl with gremolata

Minutes in the making, this is perfect for weekday suppers.

1 medium onion, peeled and
    finely chopped
1 t (5 ml) crushed fresh garlic
2 T (30 ml) olive oil
1 x 410 g can white cannellini or butter
    beans or chickpeas
pinch of ground cinnamon
½ t (2.5 ml) smoked paprika
2 cups (500 ml) peeled and
    chopped butternut
1 large ripe tomato, chopped
1 cup (250 ml) cooked rice, or
    ¼ cup (60 ml) uncooked rice
2 cups (500 ml) strong vegetable stock
handful of baby spinach leaves, torn
10 basil leaves, torn
salt and pepper
grated Parmesan and extra-virgin olive oil
    to serve

Gremolata

1 t (5 ml) crushed fresh garlic
grated zest of 1 large yellow lemon
2 T (30 ml) finely chopped Italian parsley
1 t (5 ml) extra-virgin olive oil
salt and pepper

1. Combine all the gremolata ingredients and set aside for the flavours to develop.
2. Soften the onion and garlic in the olive oil in a large saucepan over medium heat.
3. Rinse and drain the beans or chickpeas and add to the pan along with the spices, butternut, tomato, rice and stock. Cook for 15–20 minutes until tender.
4. Add the spinach and basil, stir through and put on the lid. Cook for another 10 minutes — if too liquid for your liking, remove the lid and cook at a hard boil until thickened.
5. Season to taste and serve in deep bowls garnished with a dab of gremolata and plenty of grated Parmesan, and extra-virgin olive oil drizzled over.

Serves 4

TACO SALAD

This is a light and refreshing warm-weather supper.

½ cup (125 ml) yoghurt or sour cream
1 T (15 ml) lemon juice
2 T (30 ml) olive oil
1 small fresh red chilli, chopped
½ t (2.5 ml) crushed fresh garlic
¼ t (1 ml) ground cumin
salt and pepper
80 g mixed lettuce leaves or rocket
1 red onion, peeled and thinly sliced
1 small cucumber, deseeded and chopped
200 g cherry tomatoes, halved
2 cups (500 ml) fresh or frozen corn
    kernels, lightly cooked and cooled
3 handfuls of corn nachos
1 cup (250 ml) grated Cheddar cheese
handful of fresh coriander, chopped

1. Make the dressing by whisking together the yoghurt or sour cream, lemon juice, olive oil, chilli, garlic, cumin, salt and pepper and allow to stand for 5 minutes.
2. Assemble the salad in layers as follows: lettuce leaves or rocket, onion, cucumber, tomatoes, corn, nachos and cheese.
3. Dress, garnish with chopped coriander and serve.

Serves 4

TOMATO EGG CURRY

4–8 eggs
1 medium onion, peeled and
    finely chopped
2 t (10 ml) grated fresh ginger
2 t (10 ml) crushed fresh garlic
2 t (10 ml) mild curry powder
½ t (2.5 ml) ground cinnamon
½ t (2.5 ml) ground turmeric
2 T (30 ml) sunflower oil
1 x 400 g can plain chopped tomatoes
    (or with Indian spices)
2 cups (500 ml) water
12 curry leaves
½ cup (125 ml) red lentils, rinsed
½ cup (125 ml) frozen peas
handful of fresh coriander, chopped
poppadoms and microwave spiced rice
    (see page 27) to serve

1. Place the eggs in a saucepan, cover with water and bring to the boil. As soon as the water begins to boil, put on the lid and remove the pan from the heat. Allow to stand for 15 minutes before shelling the eggs.
2. Cook the onion, ginger, garlic and spices in the oil for 3–4 minutes until aromatic. Add the tomatoes, water, curry leaves and lentils and simmer for 20 minutes until the lentils soften.
3. Add the shelled eggs and peas and simmer for 10 minutes. If the sauce becomes too thick, add ¼ cup (60 ml) water and stir well.
4. Serve garnished with coriander and with poppadoms and spiced rice.

COOK'S TIP: For low-fat poppadoms, cook individual ones on high for 18 seconds in the microwave and allow to harden before serving.

Serves 2-4

CAULIFLOWER, TOMATO AND CHICKPEA CURRY WITH MICROWAVE SPICED RICE

Cook the rice (see opposite page) while you make the curry and all will be ready in about 30 minutes. For an even faster curry, use 2 T (30 ml) bottled rogan josh or korma curry paste instead of the spices, ginger and garlic.

1 small onion, peeled and finely chopped
2 T (30 ml) oil
1 t (5 ml) crushed fresh garlic
1 t (5 ml) grated fresh ginger
½ t (2.5 ml) ground cumin
1 t (5 ml) ground coriander
1 t (5 ml) mild curry powder
1 x 410 g can chopped peeled tomatoes
1 T (15 ml) tomato concentrate
1 x 410 g can chickpeas or brown lentils,
     rinsed and drained
1 small cauliflower, broken into
     large florets
lemon atchar (see page 182) and
     chopped fresh coriander to serve

1. Fry the onion in the oil in a pot for 3–4 minutes until translucent and soft.
2. Add the garlic, ginger, cumin, coriander and curry powder and cook for another minute before adding the tomatoes, tomato concentrate and chickpeas or lentils.
3. Add the cauliflower florets and simmer for 10–15 minutes until the curry is thick and aromatic. Serve with the microwave spiced rice (see opposite page) and garnish with lemon atchar and coriander.

Serves 4

Microwave spiced rice

1 cup (250 ml) basmati rice
2 star anise
2 cardamom pods
2 bay leaves
3 whole cloves
4 cm stick cinnamon
2 cups (500 ml) water
1 t (5 ml) salt

1. Rinse the rice in a sieve under running water and combine with all the ingredients in a large Pyrex or microwaveable glass bowl. Cover with clingfilm.
2. Microwave on high for 15–20 minutes, stir well and cover again.
3. Cook for a further 5 minutes and then allow to stand covered for 5 minutes. Fluff with a fork and serve.

Serves 4

Stir-fried rice with mushrooms, sweetcorn, peas and peppers

One of the speediest suppers ever, this is a godsend for busy weekdays. Use whatever vegetables you've got to hand.

2 T (30 ml) sunflower oil
1 t (5 ml) sesame oil
½ small onion or 6 spring onions,
    finely chopped
1 t (5 ml) crushed fresh garlic
2 t (10 ml) grated fresh ginger
1 cup (250 ml) mushrooms, sliced
1 cup (250 ml) fresh or frozen
    sweetcorn kernels
½ cup (125 ml) frozen peas, thawed
1 large sweet pepper, deseeded and
    finely chopped
2 cups (500 ml) cold cooked rice
1 T (15 ml) sweet Indonesian soy sauce
½ cup (125 ml) roast cashew nuts,
    coarsely chopped
chopped fresh coriander to serve

1. Heat the oils in a wok over high heat and cook the onion until soft and translucent.
2. Add the garlic and ginger and cook for another minute before adding the vegetables.
3. Stir-fry for 5 minutes then add the rice and soy sauce. Stir well to combine and serve hot, garnished with the cashew nuts and fresh coriander.

Serves 4

2-Minute creamy spinach, chilli and tomato pasta

I came up with this recipe while in res at university. When you have some leftover cooked pasta and only a microwave, experiment with different ingredients but keep it saucy. - Jade

1 cup (250 ml) cooked pasta,
    preferably shells
½ cup (125 ml) thick cream
handful of spinach, washed, destalked
    and roughly torn
1 ripe red tomato, chopped
½ fresh chilli, chopped
salt and pepper
2 T (30 ml) grated Parmesan

1. Put the pasta, cream, spinach, tomato, chilli and seasoning in a microwaveable roasting bag or container with a lid.
2. Tie the bag and pop into the microwave for 2 minutes.
3. Pierce the bag to let the steam escape, empty the contents into a bowl, top with Parmesan and enjoy!

COOK'S TIP: Alternatively, pop all the ingredients in a pan and heat for 2 minutes over high heat so that the cream thickens.

Serves 1

MUSHROOM, CABBAGE, CELERY AND TOFU HOISIN STIR-FRY NOODLES

Chinese hoisin sauce is a nutty, sweet, dark and aromatic condiment sold in most supermarkets. It's extremely versatile and I use it in everything from marinades and rubs to salad dressings and stir-fries. Make your own version using the recipe on page 178 or buy from any reputable Asian food store. The list of ingredients seems long, but it's a very simple recipe. Prepare the tofu beforehand. - Sonia

300 g instant dried egg noodles

2 T (30 ml) peanut or sunflower oil

1 T (15 ml) sesame oil

1 small onion, peeled and sliced, or
    1 bunch spring onions, chopped

½ small green cabbage, chopped into
    2 cm chunks (about 3 cups or 750 ml)

2 t (10 ml) grated fresh ginger

1 t (5 ml) crushed fresh garlic

200 g shiitake, portabellini or button
    mushrooms, halved or quartered
    if large

2 stalks celery, diagonally sliced
    2 cm thick

2 T (30 ml) hoisin sauce (see page 178)

2 T (30 ml) soy sauce

200 g firm tofu, cubed and marinated
    in 2 T (30 ml) soy sauce and
    1 t (5 ml) grated fresh ginger
    for 15–30 minutes

1 T (15 ml) sesame seeds, toasted

1. Cook the noodles according to the packet instructions and set aside until needed. Mix a little oil through with your fingertips so they don't clump together.
2. Heat the oils together in a wok or wide frying pan over high heat. Add the onion and cook for 2–3 minutes until soft and translucent but not brown.
3. Add the cabbage, ginger and garlic and cook while stirring briskly for 3 minutes.
4. Add the mushrooms, celery and sauces and stir-fry over high heat for another 5–6 minutes, until the vegetables are cooked but still firm and crunchy.
5. Toss in the noodles, tofu and seeds, cook for another minute or two to warm through and serve hot.

Serves 4

THREE-CHEESE AND SPRING ONION BAKED POTATOES

Potatoes are best baked in a very hot oven until nicely crisp outside and floury inside but, when hunger strikes, the microwave does a creditable job. Buy large baking potatoes and use either method. Split them in half, scoop out the cooked flesh and mash with the following.

FOR EACH POTATO USE:

½ cup (125 ml) smooth cottage cheese
1 T (15 ml) grated Parmesan
1 T (15 ml) crumbled blue cheese
   (or more, to taste)
1 T (15 ml) cream
½ t (2.5 ml) crushed fresh garlic
3 spring onions, finely sliced
2 t (10 ml) chopped chives
salt and pepper

1. Scoop out the cooked potato, leaving a firm half-shell. Mash with the remaining ingredients and spoon back into each skin.
2. Place on a roasting tray and flash under a hot grill until the cheese is bubbly and golden brown. Serve with a crunchy salad of mixed leaves, sliced apple and toasted walnuts in an olive oil and lemon dressing.

ALTERNATIVE TOPPINGS:

- Mashed avocado with chilli, lemon and tahini, topped with sprouts.
- Garlic butter, black olives and chopped sundried tomatoes.
- Caramelised onion, chopped walnuts and crisp-fried sage.
- Extra-virgin olive oil, crushed garlic and lots of chopped fresh rosemary, celery salt and grated Parmesan.
- Pesto and sour cream.
- Oven-roasted courgettes and tomatoes with garlic, origanum and olive oil.
- Fried leeks, thyme and blue cheese.

Spring vegetables with parmesan cream

Steam the vegetables in a sieve positioned over a pot of cooking gnocchi or stir-fry in a little oil, whichever is easiest.

125 g asparagus spears
1 cup (250 ml) broccoli florets
125 g baby corn
1 cup (250 ml) cream
125 g sugarsnap peas
½ cup (125 ml) frozen petits
    pois, thawed
salt and pepper
dash of Tabasco sauce
3 T (45 ml) grated Parmesan
2 T (30 ml) chopped chives
2 T (30 ml) slivered almond or pine
    kernels, toasted (optional)

1. Steam or stir-fry all the vegetables, except the peas, for 4–5 minutes until just tender, then remove immediately and set aside. They should have some bite left to them.
2. Meanwhile, in a separate saucepan, bring the cream and both peas to the boil with salt, pepper and Tabasco and cook briskly until the volume has reduced by a third. Add the Parmesan and chives.
3. Toss the sauce with the vegetables, sprinkle over the almonds or pine kernels if using, and serve hot. Toss with gnocchi (see page 185) for a more substantial meal.

Serves 4

Sundried tomato, broccoli, feta and caper rigatoni

Chop, cook, steam, toss and eat. If I need steam to forge ahead during the day I make this simple pasta. – Jade

300 g dried rigatoni
12 sundried tomatoes in olive oil, chopped
    (reserve 2 T (30 ml) of the oil)
1 large head broccoli, broken into florets
    and steamed
3 wheels feta, roughly crumbled
2 T (30 ml) capers

1. Cook the pasta according to the packet instructions.
2. Stir through the reserved sundried tomato oil.
3. Add the rest of the ingredients, toss well and serve.

Serves 4

AGEDASHI TOFU

I call myself the queen of tofu dishes and this is one of my favourites. Squares of custardy tofu are dusted with cornflour, deep-fried and served in a hot savoury miso broth. Pure goodness and very, very tasty. Use firm tofu for this dish - silken tofu will disintegrate when handled. - Sonia

4 cups (1 litre) water or organic vegetable broth (see page 176)
1 piece kombu seaweed (about 7 cm)
500 g fresh firm (not silken) tofu, cut into 2 cm squares
3 T (45 ml) cornflour (use arrowroot or kuzu if you prefer)
sunflower oil for frying
3 T (45 ml) miso paste
salt
6 spring onions, very finely shredded, or chopped chives

1. Simmer the water or broth with the kombu in a saucepan for 20 minutes. Remove and discard the kombu. Keep the broth hot but not boiling.
2. Place the tofu squares on a large plate and sift over the cornflour. Roll the squares in the cornflour to coat evenly.
3. Deep-fry about six tofu squares at a time in hot sunflower oil for 5–6 minutes until golden brown on all sides. Don't overcrowd the frying pan, as this will cause the oil to cool and make the tofu squares soggy.
4. Lift out with a slotted spoon and drain each batch on absorbent paper towel.
5. Stir the miso paste into the hot broth until dissolved. Don't boil again, as this destroys the enzymes in the miso.
6. Divide the fried tofu squares between four deep bowls, pour the hot broth around them, season with salt and scatter over the spring onions. Serve immediately as a starter or as part of a larger Asian-style meal.

Serves 4

ANGEL-HAIR PASTA WITH LEMON, CAPERS AND OLIVES

This is my favourite: a delicately light and flavoursome pasta. - Jade

300 g dried linguine
grated zest and juice of 1 lemon
½ cup (125 ml) grated Parmesan
¼ cup (60 ml) extra-virgin olive oil
1 T (15 ml) capers in brine, drained
12 black olives, pitted and torn in half
8 basil leaves, torn

1. Bring a large pot of salted water to the boil and cook the pasta according to the packet instructions.
2. Whisk together the lemon zest and juice, Parmesan and olive oil until creamy. Add the capers.
3. Drain the cooked pasta and toss with the lemon cream.
4. Scatter over the olives and basil, adding a dash more olive oil if desired. Serve straightaway.

Serves 4

MICROWAVE BANANA RICE PUDDING WITH RASPBERRY JAM

This is food medicine for when life's been unkind.

1 T (15 ml) custard powder
400 ml milk (use soy or rice milk if you're
    lactose intolerant)
2 T (30 ml) caramel sugar
pinch of ground cinnamon and nutmeg
1 large very-ripe banana, chopped
85 g short-grain rice
2 T (30 ml) raspberry jam
ice-cold cream to serve

1. In a large microwaveable bowl, mix the custard powder to a paste with half the milk, then slowly stir in the rest, adding the sugar, cinnamon and nutmeg and mixing until smooth.
2. Add half the banana, cover and microwave on full power for 3 minutes.
3. Stir in the rice, cover and microwave for 6 minutes on full power.
4. Add the remaining banana, stir very well, cover and microwave for a further 4 minutes, stirring every minute to avoid clumping.
5. Allow to stand for 2 minutes before serving in bowls with a dollop of raspberry jam and a drizzle of ice-cold cream.

Serves 2

PUFF PASTRY ROUNDS WITH BERRIES AND CUSTARD CREAM

A real cheat's pudding, but who's complaining? Thaw the pastry in the fridge overnight before you need it – it will keep for up to five days.

400 g frozen puff pastry, thawed
2 T (30 ml) icing sugar
1 cup (250 ml) thick cream
1 cup (250 ml) readymade custard
350 g fresh or thawed frozen berries
¼ cup (60 ml) icing sugar for dusting

1. Preheat the oven to 200 °C. Lightly spray two baking trays with non-stick cooking spray and line with baking paper.
2. Lightly roll out the puff pastry on a floured surface and cut eight circles from it using an espresso saucer as a template. Sift over the first quantity of icing sugar.
3. Place the pastry rounds on the baking trays and bake for about 12 minutes until puffed and golden brown. Remove from the oven and cool.
4. Meanwhile, beat the cream until thick and stir in the custard.
5. When the pastry rounds are cool, set aside half. On each round, spoon over some of the custard cream, scatter over some berries and then top with one of the set aside rounds. Dust with plenty of icing sugar and serve.

Serves 4

Deconstructed tiramisu

Forgive me Italians, for putting Ferrari wheels on your classic Fiat ... this is just so fast and so good! - Jade

32 boudoir biscuits
¼ cup (60 ml) strong espresso, chilled
¼ cup (60 ml) Kahlua
1 cup (250 ml) cream, whipped to
    firm peaks
1 T (15 ml) cocoa powder for dusting

1. Arrange 4 biscuits per person on a plate and lay another four across on top.
2. Combine the espresso and Kahlua and drizzle over the biscuits. Allow to stand for 15 minutes.
3. Top with lashings of cream and dust with cocoa powder.

Serves 4

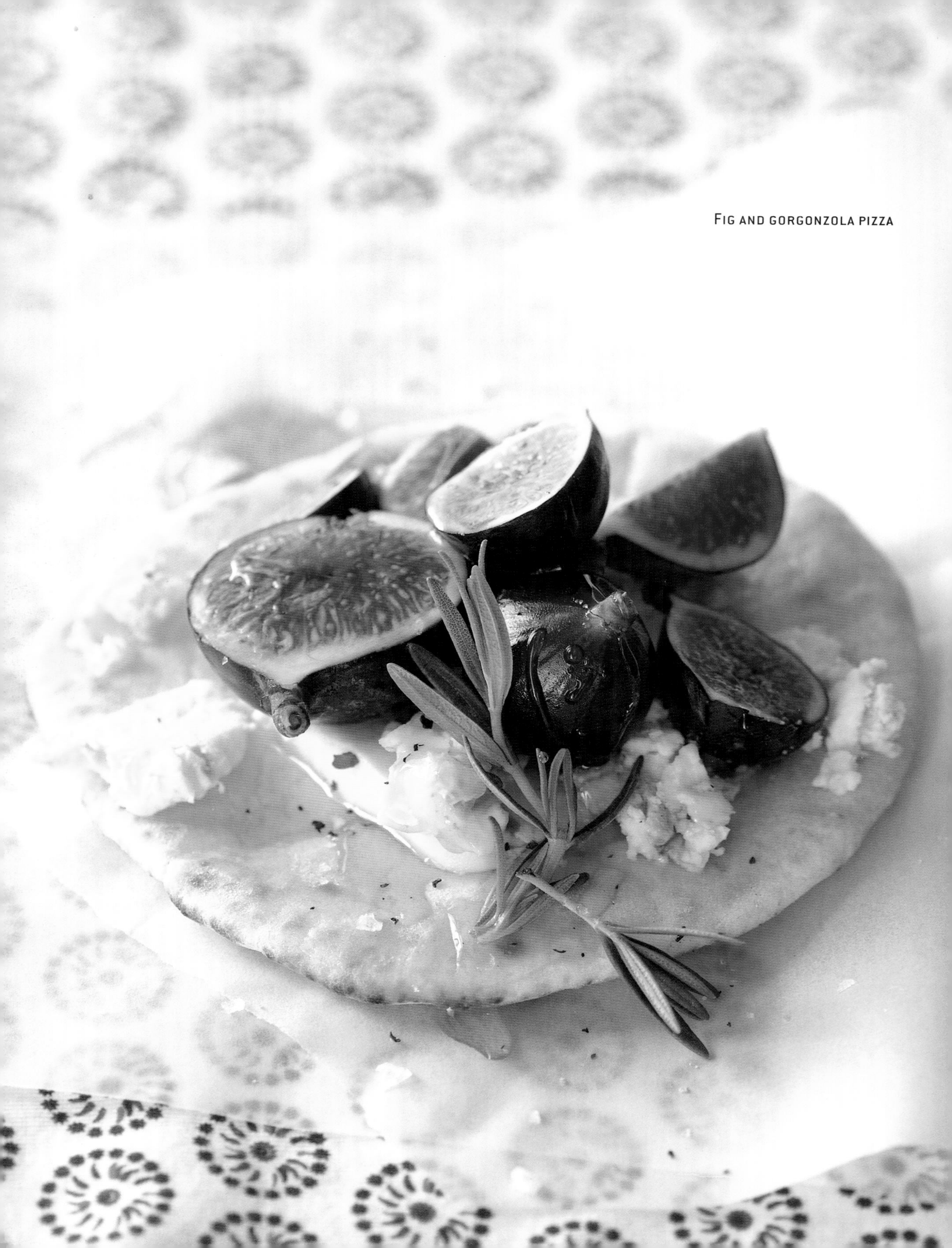

Fig and gorgonzola pizza

Light

ENERGISING BITES, SNACKS AND APPETIZERS

DRIED FRUIT AND COCONUT CHEWIES

Perfect for the holiday snack cupboard - roll in toasted coconut or sesame seeds for extra crunch. Using a food processor gets the job done in a flash.

1 large bag mixed soft dried fruit (make sure all the prunes are pitted first), roughly chopped
1 cup (250 ml) desiccated coconut or sesame seeds, toasted

1. Put all the chopped dried fruit into a blender. Make sure there are no prune stones left. Process at high speed until finely chopped and clumping together in a large ball.
2. Use clean dry hands to pinch off spoonfuls and roll into firm balls between your palms.
3. Put the coconut or sesame seeds in a medium-sized bowl and roll one chewy at a time to coat thoroughly on all sides. Pack on wax paper in airtight containers. They will keep for a month.

Makes 14-18

HONEY-ROASTED CASHEWS

Use raw almonds or raw shelled peanuts if you prefer.

250 g raw cashew nuts
½ cup (125 ml) honey
½ T (7.5 ml) Chinese five-spice powder

1. Preheat the oven to 150 °C and line two baking trays with baking paper.
2. Stir the nuts, honey and spice powder together in a saucepan over medium heat until the honey is runny and dissolved.
3. Spread the nuts in an even layer on the baking trays and roast in the oven for 15–20 minutes until golden brown. Allow to cool completely before serving.

Makes about 2 ½ cups (625 ml)

SPICED POPCORN

Each recipe makes enough for about 6 cups of freshly popped corn.

WASABI SALT WITH TOASTED SESAME SEEDS AND NORI

1 T (15 ml) wasabi powder
1 T (15 ml) sea-salt flakes
1 T (15 ml) sesame seeds, toasted
1 cup (250 ml) shredded nori strips
  (use scissors to cut sheets of nori
  into small strips)

ITALIAN

½ t (2.5ml) dried origanum
½ t (2.5ml) garlic powder
½ t (2.5ml) finely crushed
  sea-salt flakes
¼ t (1 ml) ground black pepper
¼ cup (60 ml) very finely grated
  best-quality Parmesan

HOT AND SPICY

1 T (15 ml) paprika
1 t (5 ml) onion powder
1 t (5 ml) garlic powder
2 T (30 ml) finely crushed sea-salt flakes
1 T (15 ml) ground cumin
½ T (7.5ml) cayenne pepper
¼ t (1 ml) ground black pepper

INDIAN MASALA

2 T (30 ml) mild curry powder
1 t (5 ml) ground turmeric
¼ t (1 ml) cayenne pepper
2 T (30 ml) sea-salt flakes
¼ t (1 ml) ground black pepper

POPCORN

1. Cover the base of a large heavy-bottomed saucepan with a tight-fitting lid with a thin film of sunflower oil.
2. Pour in just enough popcorn kernels to cover the base of the pot in a single layer and put on the lid.
3. Turn the heat to high and wait for the popping sounds, which will be furious at first and then start to taper off. When pops are 1 second apart, that means most of the kernels have popped.
4. Remove from the heat immediately, take off the lid and pour the popcorn into serving bowls. Toss with any of the following seasonings, made by combining all the ingredients.

Warm spiced nuts

Fresh organic nuts, lightly spiced and roasted at home are one of the most sublime treats. Always taste before you buy - rancid nut oil may be carcinogenic.

500 g fresh organic nuts (a single kind or mixed)
2 t (10 ml) sunflower oil, or 1 egg white, whisked until frothy
1 T (15 ml) smoked paprika or curry powder
1 t (5 ml) ground cumin
2 T (30 ml) crumbled nori (optional)

1. Preheat the oven to 180 °C.
2. Mix the nuts with the oil or egg white in a bowl, sprinkle over the spices and nori (if using) and mix thoroughly.
3. Spread the nuts in a single layer on baking trays and roast for 10–15 minutes in the oven.
4. Allow to cool slightly before blotting with absorbent paper towel and serving.

Serves 6-8

Banana lassi

Lassi is a refreshing Indian yoghurt drink that is served ice cold, either sweetened or salty. Vegans, use nut, soy or rice milk instead of yoghurt.

Per serving use:
400 ml cold low-fat Bulgarian yoghurt
½ cup (125 ml) frozen berries
1 small banana, chopped
2 T (30 ml) organic honey
pinch of ground cinnamon (optional)

1. Whizz all the ingredients in a blender until smooth and frothy. Serve immediately.

Cook's tip: For tangy, salty lassi, use 1 t (5 ml) dried or 1 T (15 ml) fresh chopped mint, a pinch of ground cumin or cumin seeds and ½ t (2.5 ml) salt with 400 ml cold low-fat Bulgarian yoghurt. Blend until frothy and serve immediately.

Dairy-free berry and mango smoothie

As a soothing pick-me-up in a glass or a healthy meal replacement, smoothies make great fast food using juice, milk or yoghurt as a base. Use soy, rice or nut milk if lactose intolerance is a problem.

1 cup (250 ml) milk
1 cup (250 ml) fresh or frozen raspberries or mixed berries
1 cup (250 ml) cubed mango
⅓ cup (80 ml) cold water
dash of vanilla essence

1. Whizz all the ingredients in a blender until creamy and smooth. Serve immediately.

Serves 2

ROOT CHIPS WITH TRUFFLE SALT

Truffle salt sounds terribly posh but all it really takes is a few drops of truffle oil stirred through a tablespoon or two of sea-salt flakes. Never knew you could be so grand, eh? Use a potato peeler to slice the vegetables into long thin ribbons.

6 medium parsnips, topped and peeled
2 large beetroot, peeled and sliced
    paper-thin
1 large sweet potato, peeled and sliced
    paper-thin
3 T (45 ml) olive oil
1 T (15 ml) truffle salt (as above)

1. Preheat the oven to 200 °C.
2. Toss each vegetable with 1 T (15 ml) olive oil in a bowl until well coated. Spread each vegetable on its own baking tray and sprinkle with truffle salt.
3. Roast for 15–20 minutes until nicely crisp and golden brown. Allow to cool before serving.

Serves 4

PITA PIZZAS

My freezer is never without a bag or two of frozen pitas for when hunger pangs strike, since I greatly prefer the texture to that of commercial pizza bases. Of course you're free to choose whatever base you wish, even ciabatta or French loaf works well. Spread with plain tomato purée as a base, or sliced fresh ripe tomatoes with a drizzle of garlicky olive oil, pitas make perfect pizzas. Bake at 200 °C until golden brown and crusty. - Sonia

SOME SUGGESTIONS FOR TOPPINGS:

Greek – baby spinach, sliced fresh tomato, pitted black olives, crumbled feta, torn fresh origanum and basil, crushed fresh garlic and a drizzle of olive oil

Four seasons – sliced canned artichokes, sliced mushrooms, chopped sweet peppers, pitted olives and grated mozzarella

Fig and gorgonzola – quartered fresh figs, gorgonzola, grated Parmesan, a drizzle of honey and chopped fresh rosemary

Tofu and mozzarella – sliced smoked tofu, tomato purée, ribbons of courgette, chopped fresh thyme, grated mozzarella, rocket leaves and crushed fresh garlic

Onion and brie – slow-cooked sticky balsamic onion, chopped peppadews, pitted black olives, chopped fresh rosemary and brie

Butternut and blue – roast butternut chunks, crumbled blue cheese, rocket leaves, walnuts and balsamic glaze

Thai – Thai green curry paste, sliced leeks and courgettes

CHEESY SWEET POTATO AND SESAME BALLS

A.K.A. sesame street balls, perfect for popping into your mouth - once you start it's hard to stop! These are perfect with a dab of sweet chilli sauce.

2 large sweet potatoes, peeled and cubed
2 t (10 ml) honey
1 t (5 ml) ground cinnamon
½ t (2.5 ml) ground cardamom
1 T (15 ml) cornflour
½ t (2.5 ml) salt
1 cup (250 ml) grated Cheddar cheese
½ cup (125 ml) sesame seeds, toasted
sunflower oil for deep-frying
sweet chilli sauce for dipping

1. Cook the sweet potato cubes in a little boiling water in a saucepan until very tender. Drain well and cool.
2. Mash the sweet potato with the honey, spices, cornflour and salt. Mix in the cheese.
3. Roll tablespoonfuls of the mixture into balls and roll each in sesame seeds to coat.
4. Deep-fry the balls in hot oil until golden brown. Drain on absorbent paper towel before serving with sweet chilli sauce.

Makes about 24 balls

EGGY POTATO LUNCHBOX PITAS

My athletic teenage sister's favourite pre-training snack ingredients in an easy, portable pita. - Jade

5 baby potatoes, halved
1 egg, rinsed under running water
2 gherkins, chopped
1 spring onion, chopped
3 T (45 ml) mayonnaise or
    low-fat yoghurt
handful of watercress leaves or
    alfalfa sprouts
1 wholemeal pita, toasted and top cut off

1. Cook the potato halves in boiling salted water for 5 minutes.
2. Add the whole egg in its shell and continue cooking for another 5 minutes. Drain well.
3. Shell the egg and coarsely chop.
4. Gently mix the potatoes and chopped egg with the gherkins, spring onion, mayonnaise or yoghurt and watercress or sprouts and pile into the pita.

Serves 1

CORIANDER AND SWEETCORN EGG ROLLS
WITH SWEET CHILLI SAUCE

4 eggs, beaten
½ cup (125 ml) sweetcorn kernels
2 T (30 ml) soy sauce
2 T (30 ml) water
½ t (2.5 ml) grated fresh ginger
1 t (5 ml) sesame oil
2 T (30 ml) sunflower oil
1 T (15 ml) Thai green curry paste (see
    page 177)
1 cup (250 ml) bean sprouts, rinsed
6 spring onions, shredded
handful each of fresh coriander, mint and
    basil leaves
sweet chilli sauce to serve

1. Use a fork to whisk together the eggs, sweetcorn, soy sauce, water, ginger and sesame oil.
2. Heat the sunflower oil in a small non-stick frying pan and pour in just enough egg batter to make a thin pancake. When cooked on the underside, flip over with a spatula and cook for 30 seconds on the other side. Remove and keep warm. Continue until all the batter is used up.
3. Spread each pancake with a little curry paste and then roll each one up around a filling of sprouts, onions and herbs. Cut into wheels, fasten with a toothpick and serve with sweet chilli sauce as a dip.

Serves 2

HASH BROWNS
A beloved childhood Sunday supper, served with tomato ketchup or Mrs Ball's chutney. Fancy it up with some crème fraîche and apple sauce to impress yourself.

6 medium organic potatoes, well washed
1 small onion, peeled
1 egg, well beaten
1 T (15 ml) potato flour
2 T (30 ml) chopped fresh parsley or any
    other herb
salt and freshly ground black pepper
oil for frying

1. Coarsely grate the potatoes with the peeled onion. Tip together onto a clean kitchen towel, fold the cloth around the vegetables like a Christmas cracker and wring over the sink to get rid of any excess moisture.
2. Mix the potato and onion with the remaining ingredients except the oil and stir thoroughly to combine.
3. Heat oil in a large frying pan until very hot and drop large heaped spoonfuls of hash mix into the pan. Flatten slightly with the back of a spoon while cooking.
4. Cook on both sides until brown and crispy. Drain on absorbent paper towel and serve hot.

Serves 4

INDIAN CHICKPEA PANCAKES

Use chickpea flour and serve with raita (yoghurt and cucumber dip) or fresh coriander chutney (see page 17).

1 cup (250 ml) chickpea flour, sifted
1 small red onion, peeled and very
    finely chopped
1 t (5 ml) grated fresh ginger
2 small green chillies, finely chopped
½ t (2.5 ml) salt
1 T (15 ml) crushed fresh garlic
3 T (45 ml) chopped fresh coriander
enough water to make a batter
oil for frying

1. Whizz all the ingredients except the oil together in a food processor until smooth, adding just enough water to make a batter like thick custard. The batter will keep in the fridge for up to three days; just stir well before cooking.
2. Fry spoonfuls in hot oil until golden brown on both sides and serve as suggested.

Serves 4–6

PAN FLASH OF PAPRIKA POTATO, PEPPERS AND PEAS

I like to come home to this after a night out on the tiles. – Jade

½ onion, peeled and chopped
¼ cup (60 ml) olive oil
1 medium potato, peeled and cubed
1 medium sweet red pepper, deseeded
    and sliced
pinch of sweet or smoked paprika
½ cup (125 ml) frozen peas
salt and pepper
dollop plain yoghurt or crème fraîche
handful of fresh parsley, chopped
1 pita, toasted

1. Fry the onion in the olive oil in a frying pan for 5 minutes until translucent and soft.
2. Add the potato, pepper and paprika and leave to stick to the bottom of the pan for 2 minutes.
3. Add the peas and cook for 2 more minutes before mashing with the back of a slotted spoon. Continue cooking for a further 5 minutes until the potato is soft. Season well.
4. Eat straight from the pan, with a dollop of yoghurt or crème fraîche and fresh parsley scattered over. Use the toasted pita to mop it up.

Serves 1

Mushroom burgers with feta, pesto and mozzarella

Make this vegan by omitting the cheese, adding slices of grilled aubergine (eggplant) and using vegan pesto.

4 large field mushrooms
2 T (30 ml) olive oil
salt and pepper
¼ cup (60 ml) pesto of your choice
1 wheel feta, any flavour, crumbled
1 cup (250 ml) grated mozzarella or
    8 slices brie
4 hamburger buns, halved
handful of rocket leaves

1. Preheat the oven's grill to its highest setting.
2. Brush the mushrooms with the olive oil and arrange on a roasting tray, stem side up. Season well. Grill for about 15 minutes on both sides until softened. Turn stem side up.
3. Spoon 1 T (15 ml) pesto over each mushroom, divide the cheeses evenly between them and grill for a further 3–4 minutes until the cheese is bubbling and beginning to brown.
4. Slide a mushroom onto a burger roll half, top with some rocket leaves, squash down the top of the roll and enjoy with fries and a salad.

COOK'S TIP: Use thick slices of grilled beefsteak tomato, fried halloumi or fried aubergine instead of the mushrooms.

Serves 4

FALAFEL WITH TAHINI IN PITA

Sure, falafel is not exactly flung together in a hurry, but where's the effort in soaking the chickpeas overnight? The secret is NOT to cook the chickpeas before mincing them. Use a food processor to make the entire process child's play.

FALAFEL

300 g dried organic chickpeas
1 medium onion, peeled and
    roughly chopped
handful of fresh coriander
1 T (15 ml) crushed fresh garlic
1 T (15 ml) ground coriander
½ t (2.5 ml) bicarbonate of soda
1–2 t (5–10 ml) salt
2 T (30 ml) chickpea flour
sunflower oil for frying

TAHINI SAUCE

½ cup (125 ml) plain yoghurt
2–3 T (30–45 ml) lemon juice
3 T (45 ml) tahini
salt and pepper
pinch of paprika

pitas, shredded iceberg lettuce,
    chopped tomatoes, sliced jalapeños,
    chopped onion and fresh mint to serve

1. Start the night before by rinsing the chickpeas in a sieve under running water. Place the chickpeas in a large bowl and cover with water. Leave to soak for at least 8 hours.
2. When ready to make the falafel, drain the chickpeas thoroughly and mince in a food processor with the rest of the falafel ingredients except the oil, until the mixture resembles coarse breadcrumbs. Leave to stand for 30 minutes while you make the tahini sauce.
3. To make the sauce, simply stir together all the ingredients until smooth.
4. Form tablespoonfuls of chickpea mix into firm balls by squishing and rolling them in your palms. Fry in a frying pan of oil over medium heat until brown and crisp on all sides. Drain on absorbent paper towel. Serve in pitas with the tahini sauce and all the trimmings.

Serves 4

STRAWBERRY, GINGER ALE AND MINT SLUSHY

I sold this at a market once and people still ask for it when they see me. Add tequila or vodka for a kick. - Jade

250 g strawberries, washed and hulled
2–4 T (30–60 ml) sugar, depending on
    the sweetness of the strawberries
8 cups (2 litres) cold ginger ale
handful of fresh mint
plenty of ice

1. Blend the strawberries with the sugar in a food processor.
2. Pour into a jug and add the ginger ale, mint and ice. Mix before serving.

COOK'S TIP: Alternatively, freeze the strawberry blend in ice trays and use as ice cubes in the ginger ale.

Makes 2 litres

10-MINUTE APPLE AND GINGER BISCUIT PUDDING

A favourite of mine, handed down from my grandmother Adèlé. - Jade

2 T (30 ml) butter
2 T (30 ml) sugar
6 apples, Granny Smith or Golden
    Delicious, peeled, cored and
    cut into eighths
½ t (2.5 ml) ground cinnamon
400 g ginger biscuits
2 cups (500 ml) cream
vanilla frozen yogurt to serve

1. Melt the butter and sugar in a large saucepan over low heat.
2. Add the apples and cinnamon and simmer for 5 minutes.
3. Layer the apples in a microwave-proof dish and break over half of the ginger biscuits. Pour over the cream and microwave for 3 minutes.
4. Crumble over the rest of the biscuits and serve with scoops of frozen yoghurt.

Serves 4

BRAZIL CHOCOLATE ROCKY ROADS

Use fresh nuts and mini-marshmallows, or large ones snipped into quarters with scissors.

100 g Brazil nuts, roughly chopped
    (substitute with pecan nuts or
    blanched almonds)
1 cup (250 ml) non-gelatin
    mini-marshmallows
250 g milk chocolate, chopped
200 g dark chocolate, chopped

1. Line a baking tray with a rectangle of lightly greased baking paper.
2. Mix the nuts and marshmallows in a deep bowl.
3. Melt the milk and dark chocolate together in a metal bowl suspended over a saucepan of simmering water. (Don't let the bowl touch the water; the chocolate will go grainy and spoil.)
4. Pour the melted chocolate in a steady stream over the nuts and marshmallows, stirring quickly to combine.
5. Use two spoons to scoop little mounds onto the lined tray and leave to set until firm. These will keep for 2 weeks in a cool place if stored in an airtight container.

Makes 20-24

RICOTTA PUFFS WITH HONEY AND ALMONDS

You know the feeling: you need sweet and creamy comfort in a bowl, and this is it. Serve with scoops of ice cream or as is.

450 g fresh ricotta (see page 182)
1 cup (250 ml) cake flour
1 T (15 ml) baking powder
pinch of salt
4 eggs
oil for frying
organic honey for drizzling
½ cup (125 ml) flaked almonds, toasted

1. Place the ricotta in a bowl and sift over the flour, baking powder and salt. Mash together really well before breaking the eggs into the bowl. Beat with a wooden spoon until smooth.
2. Fry teaspoonfuls of the mixture in medium-hot oil until golden brown and puffy on all sides – do not let the oil get too hot, as the puffs will scorch on the outside and be raw and runny on the inside.
3. Drain briefly on absorbent paper towel before serving warm in bowls, drizzled with some honey and topped with a scattering of toasted flaked almonds.

Serves 4-6

HOT AND SOUR SOUP WITH SHIITAKE,
TOFU AND WATERCRESS

Pure

DETOX AND REJUVENATE WITH NATURAL FOODS

BERRY AND WATERMELON CRUSH

This makes a refreshing tonic against summer blazes - chill the fruit and semi-freeze the juice for a slushy effect.

juice of 2 limes or 1 lemon
2 cups (500 ml) cubed watermelon,
    seeds and all
400 g strawberries, washed and hulled
2 cups (500 ml) diced fresh pineapple
3 cups (750 ml) cranberry juice
2 t (10 ml) grated fresh ginger

1. Liquidise all the ingredients in a food processor or blender until smooth and serve chilled.

Serves 2-4

DR JUICE

This is my favourite Saturday-morning tonic, usually bought from an eponymous market stall. Best if made with chilled ingredients. - Sonia

1 small cucumber, washed
2 green apples, washed
$1/2$ pineapple, peeled and chopped
knob fresh ginger, peeled
1 unwaxed lemon, washed and chopped,
    peel and all
1 bulb fennel, washed, leaves and all
1 small ripe avocado, chopped

1. Juice all the ingredients except the avocado.
2. Put the juice and avocado in a liquidiser or use a stick blender to blend until smooth and frothy. Serve immediately.

Serves 2

VIRGIN MARY

Rinse all the ingredients for this refreshing tomato cocktail first and chill before drinking.

6 very ripe tomatoes
1 small cucumber, peeled
3 stalks celery
1 large sweet red pepper, deseeded
3 medium carrots, peeled
8 radishes or handful of watercress
1 small unwaxed lemon, peeled and
    flesh chopped
1 T (15 ml) olive oil
pinch of cayenne pepper

1. Juice all the ingredients except the olive oil and cayenne pepper, which are stirred in just before serving.

Serves 4

SPANISH STUFFED TOMATOES

Light, refreshing and perfect for midsummer when tomatoes are at their luscious best.

8 medium ripe but firm tomatoes
½ cup (125 ml) olive oil
1 small sweet pepper, deseeded and
    finely chopped
handful of flat-leaf parsley, chopped
grated zest of ½ lemon
1 small onion, peeled and finely chopped
2 t (10 ml) crushed fresh garlic
1 small mild chilli, deseeded and finely
    chopped (optional)
1 t (5 ml) sweet paprika
2 t (10 ml) saffron threads, soaked in
    2 T (30 ml) boiling water
salt and pepper
75 g risotto rice

1. Preheat the oven to 180 °C.
2. Slice the stem ends off the tomatoes to create little caps. Use a spoon to scoop out the flesh and seeds without damaging the sides and put the shells in a roasting tin smeared with a little of the olive oil. Reserve the flesh.
3. Use a blender to purée the pepper, parsley, lemon zest, onion, garlic, chilli (if using), tomato flesh and the remaining olive oil with the paprika and saffron water. Season to taste.
4. Stir in the rice and spoon into the tomato shells, filling them to three-quarters full. Put their little caps back on and pour whatever liquid remains around the tomatoes.
5. Bake for 30–45 minutes until the rice is cooked. Serve hot or cold with a simple salad and some bread.

COOK'S TIP: Make a faster, cold version by mixing 2 cups (500 ml) cold cooked rice with chopped green olives, grated lemon zest, shredded basil, 3 T (45 ml) chopped preserved lemon, 2 T (30 ml) sultanas and 2 T (30 ml) toasted pine kernels. Season well with olive oil, salt and pepper and fill raw tomato shells.

Serves 4

Beetroot, rocket and orange soup

This is good hot or cold, garnished with some diced pickled beetroot and julienned orange zest.

2 T (30 ml) olive oil
1 medium red onion, peeled and
    finely chopped
4 large beetroot, peeled and chopped
1 stalk celery, diced
1 large potato, peeled and diced
50 g rocket leaves
julienned peel and juice of 2 oranges
    (reserve peel for garnish)
3 cups (750 ml) vegetable stock
salt and pepper

Garnish
4 t (20 ml) cold sour cream or
    Greek yoghurt
½ cup (125 ml) diced pickled beetroot

1. Add all the soup ingredients except the julienned peel to a large pot and cook for about 40 minutes until soft.
2. Remove from the heat and purée with a stick blender. Season well and serve hot or leave to chill completely before refrigerating.
3. Serve garnished with a little sour cream or Greek yoghurt, diced pickled beetroot and the julienned orange peel.

Serves 4

Gazpacho

Make this summer soother from Spanish Andalusia using tomato passata or juice, and chill for at least 4 hours for best results.

1 cucumber, peeled, deseeded
    and chopped
3 large, very ripe tomatoes, or 1 x 400 g
    can chopped tomatoes in juice
1 medium red onion, peeled and chopped
1 green sweet pepper, deseeded
    and chopped
2 t (10 ml) crushed fresh garlic
¼ cup (60 ml) fresh white breadcrumbs
1 cup (250 ml) cold water
1 cup (250 ml) tomato juice or passata
1 T (15 ml) red wine vinegar
1 T (15 ml) lemon juice
¼ cup (60 ml) extra-virgin olive oil
1 t (5 ml) tomato concentrate
salt and pepper

Garnish
2 T (30 ml) each of diced peeled
    cucumber, onion and green or red
    sweet pepper
¼ cup (60 ml) croutons

1. Combine all the soup ingredients in a large bowl and allow to stand for 30 minutes. Then process cupfuls at a time until smooth. Stir well, cover and refrigerate until very cold.
2. Taste for seasoning as cold dulls the taste. Serve in chilled bowls with some of the garnish sprinkled over.

Serves 4-6

HOT AND SOUR SOUP WITH SHIITAKE, TOFU AND WATERCRESS

6 cups (1.5 litres) strong vegetable stock
4 slices fresh ginger
1 stalk lemongrass
3 T (45 ml) dark soy sauce
5 T (75 ml) rice vinegar
2 t (10 ml) sesame oil
4 fresh or rehydrated dried shiitake
    mushrooms, thinly sliced
250–300 g firm tofu, cubed
1 small Thai chilli, finely sliced
50 g watercress, chopped
4 spring onions, finely sliced on
    the diagonal

1. Simmer the stock with the ginger and lemongrass in a large pot for 20 minutes and then scoop out the ginger and lemongrass.
2. Season the soup with the soy sauce, rice vinegar and sesame oil, add the mushrooms and cook for 5 minutes.
3. Divide the tofu, chilli, watercress and spring onions between deep bowls and pour over the hot soup. Serve immediately.

Serves 4-6

QUICK PEA AND GREEN APPLE SOUP WITH TARRAGON YOGHURT

This soup is a vivid emerald green, and is delicious hot or cold. Use frozen petits pois.

8 spring onions, white parts only, very
    thinly sliced
2½ cups (625 ml) frozen peas
2 Granny Smith apples, peeled, cored
    and chopped
2 T (30 ml) unsalted butter or olive oil
4 cups (1 litre) vegetable stock
salt and ground white pepper
2 T (30 ml) Greek yoghurt
1 t (5 ml) dried or chopped fresh tarragon

1. Cook the spring onions, peas and apples in the butter or olive oil in a large pot over medium heat for 10 minutes.
2. Add the stock and seasoning and simmer for 15–20 minutes over a gentle heat.
3. Use a stick blender to liquidise and serve with a little yoghurt and tarragon as garnish.

Serves 4

Grilled nectarine, buffalo mozzarella and rocket

2 firm, ripe nectarines
1 ball buffalo mozzarella
½ cup (125 ml) pecan nuts, lightly
    toasted and snapped in half
100 g rocket leaves
olive oil and balsamic vinegar or vino
    cotto for dressing
salt and pepper

1. Heat a griddle pan until very hot. Halve and stone the nectarines and grill cut-side down until lightly charred.
2. Tear the mozzarella ball into chunks, toss with the pecan nuts, rocket leaves and grilled nectarines in a serving bowl and dress lightly with olive oil and balsamic vinegar or vino cotto. Season and serve.

Serves 4

Fresh fig, asparagus and pomegranate salad

If you're lucky enough to find fresh white and green asparagus in season, use both. The colours of this salad are sensational.

24 fresh asparagus spears (green, white
    or half/half of each)
2 x 120 g pillow packs baby leaf and
    herb salad
handful of mixed fresh herbs: chervil,
    basil, dill, mint, chives and parsley
handful of beetroot sprouts (optional)
8 ripe figs, wiped clean
1 cup (250 ml) Rosa tomatoes
2 logs chèvre (goat's cheese) in black
    pepper, broken into chunks
½ cup (125 ml) pomegranate rubies
fruity extra-virgin olive oil and aged
    balsamic vinegar for dressing
salt and pepper

1. Trim the stems of the asparagus spears and blanch each kind separately in plenty of salted boiling water until just tender – no more than 3 minutes. Remove and immediately plunge into iced water for 20 seconds to stop cooking and retain colour and texture. Cool completely.
2. To serve, arrange the leaves and herbs on plates and then divide the remaining ingredients evenly between four plates. Drizzle with olive oil and balsamic vinegar, season and serve immediately.

Serves 4

Gluten-free wraps with bean chilli, brown rice, carrots, peppers and guacamole

The list of ingredients may seem long, but trust us when we say this recipe is the ultimate in speed and ease. Set the accompaniments out in little bowls for everyone to help themselves. Some like their guacamole - or Mexican avocado dip - smooth, some like it chunky. Mash or chop, it's up to you. Classic with tomato salsa and nachos.

Bean chilli

1 large onion, peeled and finely chopped
1 T (15 ml) crushed fresh garlic
2 T (30 ml) olive oil
2 T (30 ml) smoked paprika
2 T (30 ml) ground cumin
2 T (30 ml) red wine vinegar
2 T (30 ml) brown sugar
2 x 400 g cans red kidney beans, rinsed
    and drained
2 x 400 g cans chopped tomatoes,
    any flavour
salt and pepper

Guacamole

1 large ripe avocado, peeled and chopped
    or mashed
1 small tomato, deseeded and
    finely chopped
1 small red onion, peeled and very
    finely chopped
2 T (30 ml) finely chopped fresh
    coriander, leaves only
1 T (15 ml) fresh lime or lemon juice
1 T (15 ml) red wine vinegar
1 small green chilli, deseeded and very
    finely minced
½ t (2.5 ml) salt
ground black pepper

4–6 gluten-free wraps
2 cups (500 ml) cooked brown rice or
    other grain
2 cups julienned carrots
1 large sweet pepper, deseeded and cut
    into strips
6 radishes, thinly sliced

1. To make the bean chilli, cook the onion and garlic in the olive oil in a pot until the onion is soft.
2. Add the spices, cook for a further 3 minutes, then add the vinegar, sugar, beans and tomatoes. Simmer for 15–20 minutes until thick. Season well.
3. To make the guacamole, mix all the ingredients together using a fork, until very well incorporated. Taste for seasoning and adjust. Keep cold until needed, but use on the day of making.
4. Serve the bean chilli with wraps, accompaniments and the guacamole for everyone to roll their own.

Serves 4–6

CAPONATA

Make this in summer when aubergines (eggplants) and tomatoes are abundant, cheap and at their best. It is a tangy sweet and sour Sicilian speciality that keeps for several days in the fridge.

3 large aubergines, washed and chopped
    into chunks
¾ cup (180 ml) olive oil
2 red onions, peeled and thinly sliced
4 large ripe tomatoes, quartered
2 t (10 ml) capers, drained and rinsed
3 T (45 ml) sultanas
4 stalks celery, chopped
50 ml red wine vinegar
salt and pepper
2 T (30 ml) pine kernels, toasted
fresh crusty bread to serve

1. Slowly cook the aubergines in the olive oil in a large frying pan until soft. Remove with a slotted spoon and set aside. Add the onions and cook slowly over low heat until soft and translucent.
2. Add the tomatoes and cook until they collapse, before adding the aubergines and the remaining ingredients except the pine kernels. Season well and cook for 20 minutes.
3. Stir in the pine kernels and allow to cool before serving with crusty bread.

Serves 4

ROAST PEAR, PECAN AND CRANBERRY SALAD WITH HONEY AND SESAME VINAIGRETTE

Satisfy your craving for sweet, tangy and crunchy with pure, healthy ingredients.

4 pears, cored and quartered
100 g organic pecan nuts
1 T (15 ml) olive oil (use hazelnut or
    walnut oil if you have)
salt and pepper
4 handfuls of crunchy Italian salad mix
    with some bitter leaves like endive
    and radicchio
¾ cup (180 ml) dried cranberries

HONEY AND SESAME VINAIGRETTE
2 T (30 ml) honey
¼ cup (60 ml) red wine vinegar
1 T (15 ml) sesame oil
1 T (15 ml) sesame seeds, toasted
3 T (45 ml) olive oil
salt and pepper

1. Preheat the oven to 200 °C. Put the pear slices and pecan nuts on a baking tray and drizzle lightly with the olive oil. Season lightly and roast until the pears and nuts are golden brown. (You will have to remove the nuts before the pears, otherwise they'll scorch.)
2. Whisk together all the vinaigrette ingredients.
3. Arrange the salad mix, pears, nuts and cranberries on plates, drizzle over the dressing and serve.

Serves 4

CHICORY, WILTED RED ONION AND WHITE BEAN SALAD

Add grilled halloumi slices to make this a more substantial meal.

2 x 410 g cans cannellini or white
    kidney beans
3 T (45 ml) red wine vinegar
½ t (2.5 ml) salt
2 medium red onions, peeled and very
    thinly sliced
1 T (15 ml) Dijon mustard
100 ml extra-virgin olive oil
salt and pepper
4 large handfuls of Italian salad leaf mix
    with bitter leaves like chicory, curly
    endive and radicchio
12 green olives, chopped, or 1 T (15 ml)
    capers in brine, rinsed and patted dry
12 sundried tomato halves, snipped
    into strips

1. Rinse and drain the beans and set aside.
2. Pour the vinegar and salt over the sliced onions and allow to stand for 20 minutes. Drain, reserving the vinegar.
3. Whisk the reserved vinegar with the mustard, olive oil and seasoning (remember it's got salt in it already) until creamy.
4. Arrange the leaves on plates, scatter over the olives or capers, sundried tomatoes and onions, spoon over the beans and drizzle with the dressing.

Serves 4

WATERMELON CARPACCIO WITH AVOCADO, RED ONIONS AND OLIVES

This is summer loving on a plate – use watermelons when they are at their sweetest. I sometimes cut the watermelon into little hearts if I want to show some love. – Jade

¼ small watermelon, chilled
1 red onion, peeled
1 avocado
½ cup (125 ml) black olives, pitted
handful of baby leaves or wild rocket
juice of ½ lemon
2 T (30 ml) extra-virgin olive oil
salt and freshly ground black pepper

1. Slice the watermelon as thin as possible, carpaccio-style, and arrange on a serving plate.
2. Slice the red onion thinly in rings, separate and scatter over the watermelon to create a layered effect.
3. Halve the avocado and scoop out the flesh with a spoon onto the onion.
4. Scatter over the olives and pile the leaves in the centre.
5. Mix the lemon juice, olive oil, salt and pepper and pour over the salad.

Serves 4

LEAF WRAPS

To ease off the weekend's excesses and sail into the week, my mom and I decided to eat 'raw' every Monday. It soon became quite a challenge - how to keep the flavours and textures exciting, energy and humour levels high and taste buds from feeling 'cooked'? The answer lies wrapped up in this recipe. - Jade

2 large cos lettuce or spinach leaves
1 avocado, sliced
½ juicy ripe tomato, diced
6 olives, pitted and flesh torn in half
handful of chickpea sprouts
handful of coriander leaves
sea-salt flakes or gomasio (see page 185)

1. Choose two leaves each about the size of your palm; rinse, dry and place on a plate.
2. Layer with the avocado, tomato, olives and, lastly, the sprouts and coriander. Season, roll up and snack away!

Serves 1

VIETNAMESE ASPARAGUS WITH PINEAPPLE, COCONUT MILK AND ROAST PEANUTS

Using low-fat coconut milk makes this a guilt-free treat - serve with glass noodles for a tasty snack.

450 g fresh asparagus spears,
    stalks trimmed
1 pineapple, peeled and chopped into
    2 cm chunks
2 t (10 ml) crushed fresh garlic
1 small red onion, peeled and
    finely chopped
½ can (200 ml) low-fat or light
    coconut milk
½ t (2.5 ml) sugar
1 small red chilli, halved diagonally
2 T (30 ml) sesame oil
2 T (30 ml) chopped fresh mint
¼ cup (60 ml) roasted shelled peanuts

1. Place all the ingredients except the mint and peanuts in a saucepan and simmer for 10 minutes until just tender.
2. Sprinkle over the mint and peanuts and serve hot over glass noodles.

Serves 4

Sweet and sour bulgur with beetroot, spinach, feta, apricots, pumpkin seeds and sultanas

This is a jolly, colourful rainbow of a dish with heaps of taste and texture.

2 T (30 ml) orange juice

1 T (15 ml) red wine vinegar

¼ cup (60 ml) olive oil

salt and pepper

1 cup (250 ml) bulgur or couscous,
   prepared according to package
   instructions, or dehusked millet
   cooked in 2 cups (500 ml) vegetable
   stock until fluffy

4–6 small pickled beetroot, diced

large handful of baby spinach leaves,
   destalked and torn

2 wheels feta, crumbled

6 soft dried apricots, snipped
   with scissors

2 T (30 ml) pumpkin seeds

2 T (30 ml) sultanas

1. Whisk together the juice, vinegar, olive oil and seasoning and set aside.
2. Toss the remaining ingredients together, drizzle over the dressing and serve at room temperature.

Serves 4

Thai cucumber salad

*Asian salad dressings generally contain no oil, but you can add
1 T (15 ml) sesame oil for flavour.*

2 t (10 ml) sugar or honey

1 T (15 ml) lime juice

1 T (15 ml) sesame seeds, toasted

1 small cucumber, halved lengthways,
   deseeded and sliced

2 handfuls (about 150 g) of bean
   sprouts, rinsed

4 spring onions, finely sliced

1 small red chilli, finely sliced

1 cup (250 ml) shredded green cabbage

handful each of fresh mint, coriander and
   basil leaves

½ cup (125 ml) roasted peanuts,
   coarsely chopped

1. Dissolve the sugar or honey in the lime juice and stir in the sesame seeds.
2. Combine all the salad ingredients and toss with the dressing. Serve immediately.

Serves 4

THAI GREEN VEGETABLE CURRY

Make the most of tender young vegetables with this recipe, which bathes just-cooked vegetables in a lightly spiced low-fat coconut milk. Serve with rice or rice noodles.

2 cups (500 ml) low-fat coconut milk
1 T (15 ml) Thai green curry paste
    (see page 177)
4 lime leaves
1 medium red chilli, sliced in
    half diagonally
1 T (15 ml) palm or soft brown sugar
handful of fine green beans, topped
    and tailed
8 patty pans, thickly sliced
8 baby corn spears, sliced in
    half diagonally
4–6 baby aubergines (eggplants), halved
12 asparagus spears, cut in 3 cm lengths
handful of sugarsnap peas
8 cherry tomatoes, halved
handful of fresh coriander leaves

1. Simmer the coconut milk with the curry paste, lime leaves, chilli and sugar in a pot for 5–7 minutes before adding all the vegetables all at once.
2. Bring to the boil and cook quickly for 10–12 minutes, until the vegetables are just tender. Garnish with coriander and serve hot.

Serves 4

SAVOURY ASIAN SCRAMBLED TOFU WITH MUSHROOMS AND PEPPERS

Use fresh, firm tofu for this light but filling dish.

600 g fresh firm tofu
2 T (30 ml) sesame oil
1 small red onion, peeled and very
    finely chopped
1 t (5 ml) grated fresh ginger
6 shiitake or portabellini
    mushrooms, chopped
1 small red pepper, diced
1 T (15 ml) tamari or light soy sauce
1 small green chilli, finely chopped, or a
    little freshly ground black pepper
chopped fresh coriander, mint and chives
    to garnish

1. Wrap the tofu in a clean kitchen towel and place on a plate. Put another plate on top and weigh down with a 410 g can of beans for 10 minutes to extract as much moisture as possible.
2. Heat the sesame oil in a frying pan and cook the onion, ginger, mushrooms and red pepper over medium heat for about 4 minutes until softened.
3. Crumble the tofu into the pan and add the tamari and chilli. Cook while stirring for another 3 minutes to blend well. Serve hot or cold, garnished with the chopped fresh herbs.

Serves 4

Wild rice mushroom bowl

⅔ cup (160 ml) wild rice
1½ cups (375 ml) vegetable stock
1 medium onion, peeled and
    finely chopped
1 t (5 ml) crushed fresh garlic
1 T (15 ml) olive oil or butter
300 g mixed mushrooms, sliced
1 t (5 ml) dried thyme
1 t (5 ml) dried origanum
2 bay leaves
1 cup (250 ml) basmati rice
2 cups (500 ml) vegetable stock
2 T (30 ml) chopped fresh parsley
1 T (15 ml) pine kernels or
    almonds, toasted

1. Cook the wild rice in the first amount of stock for about 35 minutes until very tender. Drain and set aside.
2. Cook the onion and garlic in the olive oil or butter in a large pot until soft and translucent, and then add the mushrooms, herbs and basmati rice.
3. Stir over high heat for 5 minutes to coat the rice. Pour in the second amount of stock, put on the lid and bring to the boil. Turn down the heat and simmer until the rice is cooked and tender.
4. Stir in the wild rice, parsley and pine kernels or almonds and serve hot.

Serves 4

Red lentil and carrot dhal with coconut rice

Dhal is the staple diet of many millions on earth. The word can refer to any of the large variety of lentils, or the cooked dish itself, which is often quite soupy and eaten almost like a sauce over rice. The list of ingredients seems long, but it's done in a flash.

1 cup (250 ml) red lentils, thoroughly
    rinsed in a sieve held under
    running water
2 cups (500 ml) water
1 t (5 ml) salt
1 small carrot, peeled and finely grated
½ t (2.5 ml) ground turmeric
½ t (2.5 ml) crushed fresh garlic
½ t (2.5 ml) ground cumin
1 t (5 ml) lemon juice

Coconut rice
1 cup (250 ml) basmati rice, thoroughly
    rinsed in a sieve held under
    running water
1 cup (250 ml) low-fat coconut milk
1 cup (250 ml) water
1 t (5 ml) salt

1. Combine all the ingredients in a saucepan and bring to the boil. Simmer for about 20 minutes until the lentils are very soft and the consistency of runny porridge. Stir briskly to break up the lentils and make them creamier.
2. Meanwhile, cook the coconut rice: combine the rice, coconut milk, water and salt in a saucepan, cover and bring to the boil. Boil for 10 minutes, turn down the heat to low and simmer gently until all the liquid is absorbed. Turn off the heat without removing the lid and allow to stand for 10 minutes to soften. Fluff up with a fork and serve with the dhal.

Serves 2-4

Gluten-free asian noodles with ginger, sesame, honey and chilli

From start to finish, this takes about 15 minutes and tastes superb.

300 g soba, buckwheat or rice noodles

2 T (30 ml) rice vinegar

3 T (45 ml) light soy sauce

2 T (30 ml) honey

1–2 t (5–10 ml) chilli paste or chopped
fresh chillies

2 T (30 ml) minced fresh ginger

2 T (30 ml) sesame oil

2 T (30 ml) snipped chives or chopped
spring onion

2 T (30 ml) chopped fresh coriander

1 T (15 ml) sesame seeds, toasted

100 g honey-roasted cashews,
roughly chopped

1. Cook the noodles according to the packet instructions.
2. While the noodles are cooking, mix the remaining ingredients, except the seeds and nuts, in a large bowl, stir well and set aside to infuse.
3. Drain the noodles and toss through the sauce. Allow to stand for 5 minutes for the flavours to absorb, then scatter over the seeds and nuts and serve warm or at room temperature.

Serves 4

Tofu larb in lettuce cups

Larb is a Thai snack traditionally made with very finely minced duck, chicken or pork. I've devised a fabulous version using firm tofu. All of the pleasure with none of the guilt. – Sonia

3 T (45 ml) soy sauce

1 T (15 ml) grated fresh ginger

3 T (45 ml) lime juice

400 g firm tofu, cubed

1 T (15 ml) peanut oil

1 T (15 ml) finely minced lemongrass
(use tender inner part of stem only)

1 t (5 ml) crushed fresh garlic (optional)

¾ cup (180 ml) mint leaves,
finely chopped

½ cup (125 ml) coriander
leaves, chopped

5 fresh lime leaves, finely
shredded (optional)

1 small red onion, peeled and very
finely chopped

2 small red chillies, deseeded and
finely chopped

4 gem lettuces or 1 iceberg, split into
individual leaves, rinsed and dried

½ cup (125 ml) roasted peanuts, chopped

1. Pour the soy sauce, ginger and lime juice over the tofu and marinate for 30 minutes.
2. Heat the peanut oil in a pan over medium heat and cook the tofu, stirring quite vigorously so it crumbles, for about 10 minutes.
3. Remove from the heat and scoop into a glass dish. Cool completely before mixing very well with the remaining ingredients except the lettuce and peanuts.
4. Serve by spooning some larb into a lettuce leaf, sprinkle over some peanuts and munch away.

Serves 4

AUBERGINE ROLLS BAKED WITH HALLOUMI, ROCKET AND RED PEPPERS

1 x 410 g can chopped peeled tomatoes,
    plain or seasoned
¼ cup (60 ml) olive oil
salt and pepper
2 medium aubergines (eggplants)
¼ cup (60 ml) tahini
1 large or 2 medium red sweet
    peppers, deseeded
200 g halloumi
50 g rocket leaves
¼ cup (60 ml) basil pesto
¼ cup (60 ml) breadcrumbs or grated
    Parmesan, or both

1. Preheat the oven to 200 °C. Lightly grease a baking tray.
2. Pour the can of tomatoes and 3 T (45 ml) of the olive oil into a baking dish and season. Set aside.
3. Slice the aubergines lengthways into 75 mm-thick slices. Brush lightly on both sides with the remaining olive oil, season and roast on the greased baking tray for about 15 minutes until golden brown. Remove and cool, but leave the oven on.
4. Brush one side of each aubergine slice with tahini.
5. Cut the peppers and halloumi into strips about 5 mm thick.
6. Place a few strips of pepper and halloumi horizontally across the thin end of each aubergine slice, add a few rocket leaves and a little drizzle of pesto.
7. Roll up the aubergine slices around the filling and place in the baking dish with the tomatoes. Sprinkle over the breadcrumbs or Parmesan and bake for 35–40 minutes until golden brown.

Serves 4

ORANGES IN ORANGE FLOWER WATER

This is a citrusy Moroccan treat to serve as a salad or dessert. Use naartjies, blood oranges, navels, ruby grapefruit or even a mixture of them all. I like a garnish of fresh mint and pomegranate rubies. - Sonia

4 medium oranges, peeled, all pith and
    outer membrane sliced away with a
    very sharp knife, flesh sliced very
    thinly across
½ t (2.5 ml) orange flower water
2 t (10 ml) icing sugar
¼ t (1 ml) ground cinnamon
handful of fresh mint leaves
¼ cup (60 ml) pomegranate rubies

1. Arrange the orange slices on a decorative platter, sprinkle over the orange flower water and refrigerate until very cold.
2. To serve, mix the icing sugar and cinnamon, dust lightly over the oranges, and garnish with mint and pomegranate rubies.

Serves 4

CELERY, APPLE, ASPARAGUS AND FENNEL SALAD WITH LEMON DILL DRESSING

15 asparagus spears
2 medium Red Gala apples, thinly sliced
    and drizzled with lemon olive oil
4 stalks celery with leaves from inside of
    bunch, chopped
2 medium fennel bulbs, very thinly sliced
1 T (15 ml) lemon juice
3 T (45 ml) olive oil
1 T (15 ml) chopped fresh dill fronds
celery salt and pepper
½ cup (125 ml) pecan nuts,
    toasted (optional)

1. Place the asparagus spears in a bowl and cover with boiling water. Allow to stand for 15 minutes, then drain and leave to cool – the spears will be tender with some crunchiness remaining.
2. Arrange the asparagus, apples, celery and fennel attractively on plates.
3. Whisk together the lemon juice, olive oil, dill and seasoning and pour over the salads. Garnish with pecan nuts, if using, and serve straightaway.

Serves 4

TOMATO, OLIVE AND LEMON SALAD

Make the most of summer's ripe red tomatoes with this easy recipe.

6 plum tomatoes, quartered
handful of black olives, stoned and torn
    in half
handful of fresh flat-leaf parsley, rinsed
    and roughly chopped
2 small red onions, peeled and
    thinly sliced
grated zest and juice of 1 lemon
¼ cup (60 ml) olive oil
salt and pepper

1. Combine all the ingredients and allow to stand for 15 minutes for the flavours to marry.

Serves 4

SPICED PITA NACHOS WITH AVOCADO AND TOMATO SALSA

Commercial nachos can be very high in salt and fat. These chips are easy to make and go well with any kind of dip. This is a nice way to use up slightly stale pitas too.

⅓ cup (80 ml) olive oil
1 t (5 ml) crushed fresh garlic
6 wholewheat or plain pitas, split in
    half horizontally
1 t (5 ml) each of coriander and cumin
    seeds, dry-roasted and finely crushed
2 t (10 ml) dried Italian herbs
2 t (10 ml) sea-salt flakes
guacamole (see page 71)

AVOCADO AND TOMATO SALSA
1 ripe avocado, chopped
1 large ripe tomato, deseeded and
    finely diced
1 red chilli, seeded and minced
1 small red onion, peeled and finely diced
1 T (15 ml) chopped fresh coriander
1 T (15 ml) lime or lemon juice
salt and pepper

1. Preheat the oven to 180 °C.
2. Mix the oil and garlic in a small bowl.
3. Brush both sides of each pita with the garlic oil and cut each into 8 wedges.
4. Lightly sprinkle the pitas with the spices, herbs and salt and spread out on a baking tray.
5. Toast for about 10 minutes until golden brown and crisp. Allow to cool.
6. Stir together the salsa ingredients and spoon into a serving bowl. Serve with the guacamole and pita chips.

Serves 4-6

LENTIL, POTATO AND AUBERGINE MOUSSAKA

3 medium-sized aubergines
    (eggplants), sliced lengthways
    into 1 cm-thick slices
100 ml olive oil
salt and pepper
2 large onions, peeled and very
    finely chopped
2 t (10 ml) crushed fresh garlic
2 x 410 g cans chopped peeled tomatoes
1 x 420 g can tomato purée
1 t (5 ml) dried origanum
½ t (2.5 ml) ground cinnamon
3 cups (750 ml) cooked brown
    lentils, drained
6 large cooked floury potatoes, peeled
    and sliced lengthways 1 cm thick
½ cup (125 ml) crumbled feta or grated
    halloumi or Parmesan cheese

WHITE SAUCE
450 ml warm milk
3 T (45 ml) butter
3 T (45 ml) cake flour
salt and pepper
3 eggs

1. Preheat the oven to 180 °C.
2. Brush each aubergine slice with a little olive oil, season and roast on baking trays until golden brown and tender. Set aside.
3. Cook the onions and garlic in the remaining olive oil in a large frying pan for 6–7 minutes until soft and translucent.
4. Add all the tomatoes and tomato purée at once with the origanum and cinnamon, and stir well. Cook over medium heat for about 20 minutes until thick and aromatic.
5. Meanwhile, make the white sauce: warm the milk and butter in a saucepan until the butter melts, whisk in the flour and cook while stirring for about 5 minutes. Lower the heat, season and cook gently for 15 minutes until the sauce is thick. Remove from the heat and beat in the eggs until thoroughly blended.
6. Assemble the moussaka by alternately layering tomato and onion sauce, aubergine slices, cooked lentils, potato slices and white sauce in an ovenproof dish, repeating the layers until all is used up.
7. Finish with a layer of white sauce, sprinkle over the cheese and bake at 180 °C for 45 minutes until golden brown on top. Allow to rest for 15 minutes before serving.

Serves 6-8

COOK'S TIP: For the floury potatoes: cook potatoes whole in cold water for 10 minutes and then slice.

BERRY YOGHURT BRÛLÉE

Feast

SEASONAL FEASTS AND CELEBRATIONS

Brunch

VODKA SMOOTHIE WITH PINEAPPLE, COCONUT AND LIME

For best results, chill all the ingredients before blending.

2 cups (500 ml) pineapple juice or
    crushed pineapple in juice
¾ cup (180 ml) low-fat coconut milk
1 small banana, chopped
zest and juice of 1 lime
4 tots (100 ml) vodka
¼ cup (60 ml) castor sugar
1 cup (250 ml) ice cubes

1. Put all the ingredients in a blender and blend at high speed until smooth and frothy. Serve in tall, chilled glasses.

Serves 4

MOJITO GRANITA

Allow a couple of hours for freezing.

handful of fresh mint leaves
2 T (30 ml) castor sugar
1 cup (250 ml) fresh lime juice
    (about 5 limes)
6 tots (150 ml) white rum
1 cup (250 ml) cold water
slices of lime to garnish

1. Crush the mint leaves with the castor sugar using a pestle and mortar or in a liquidiser.
2. Add the liquids and process until smooth.
3. Freeze in a shallow plastic tray. Once frozen, bash it up a little with the back of a spoon into a slushy granita and serve in chilled glasses, garnished with a slice of lime.

Serve 4-6

WHITE SANGRIA

Everyone knows red wine sangria, but I prefer this zesty sparkling version for summer. – Sonia

1 bottle dry white wine, like
    Sauvignon Blanc
1 bottle sparkling wine
6 tots (150 ml) vodka, white rum
    or tequila
2 cups (500 ml) seedless green
    grapes, halved
1 large red apple, thinly sliced
1 orange, all peel and pith sliced away
    and flesh thinly sliced
1 large bottle Appletiser or lemonade,
    well chilled
½ cup (125 ml) fresh mint leaves
plenty of ice cubes

1. Pour the alcohol over the prepared fruit in a large bowl and refrigerate until very cold.
2. Add the Appletiser, mint and ice cubes and serve in chilled glasses.

Serve 6-8

Ruby grapefruit campari

4 cups (1 litre) ruby grapefruit juice
120 ml vodka
120 ml Campari
crushed ice
fresh mint leaves to garnish

1. Combine all the ingredients and serve in tall, frosted glasses garnished with fresh mint.

Serves 4

Berry yoghurt brûlée
Wickedly decadent toffee marries the virtuous allure of berries and yoghurt. We dare you not to succumb.

3 cups (750 ml) thick vanilla or Greek yoghurt, very well chilled
400 g mixed fresh berries of any kind, well chilled
2 nectarines, chilled and sliced
1 cup (250 ml) castor sugar
1 cup (250 ml) water

1. Spoon the yoghurt into an attractive serving dish and arrange the berries and nectarine slices on top, covering the entire surface.
2. Stir the sugar and water together in a medium saucepan over high heat. Stop stirring once the sugar has melted, and watch carefully as it begins to turn first golden, then amber and then caramel brown. When you smell the distinctive aroma of caramel, quickly remove from the heat and carefully pour all over the berries and nectarines. Serve straightaway. Sinfully good!

Serves 6-8

Truffled mushrooms on toast
Omit the egg for a vegan version. This is best made with a variety of exotic mushrooms, although portabellini and buttons work very well.

300 g mixed exotic mushrooms or any other kind, chopped
2 T (30 ml) olive oil
1 T (15 ml) finely chopped fresh rosemary sprigs
4 sage leaves, finely chopped
salt and pepper
4 slices wholewheat toast, buttered
4 large eggs
handful of rocket leaves
Parmesan shavings to garnish
4–8 drops truffle oil

1. Cook the mushrooms in half the olive oil with the rosemary, sage and seasoning until all the moisture has evaporated. Remove with a slotted spoon and divide between the slices of buttered toast.
2. Fry the eggs in the remaining olive oil until done to taste.
3. Slide onto the mushrooms and garnish with rocket leaves, shavings of Parmesan and a drop or two of truffle oil. Serve immediately.

Serves 4

JADE'S MINI BREAKFAST FRITTATAS

These mini-mouthfuls are magnificent show-stoppers at the breakfast table and are easier to serve than big frittatas.

6 eggs
2 T (30 ml) full-fat milk
salt and pepper

FILLING SUGGESTIONS
peas, mint and cooked asparagus tips
grated mozzarella, tomato and basil
sliced par-boiled potatoes and paprika
olives, diced red onions and feta

1. Preheat the oven to 180 °C. Grease 4 holes in a muffin tin.
2. Beat the eggs, milk and seasoning in a bowl. Pour the egg mixture into the muffin tin, filling the holes three-quarters full.
3. Top with fillings of your choice.
4. Bake for 10–12 minutes or until just set. Serve warm or at room temperature.

Serves 4

SWEET POTATO PANCAKES WITH AVOCADO, LIME, CORIANDER AND SAUTÉED PEPPERS

Sweet potato cooks down into a pulp very fast, but it needs to cool to make this batter. Try to find sweet potatoes with pink or yellow flesh for a rosy effect.

250 g sweet potato, peeled and chopped
    into chunks
3 T (45 ml) oil, plus extra for frying
1 cup (250 ml) milk (use soy or rice milk
    for a vegan version)
½ t (2.5 ml) grated fresh ginger
2 t (10 ml) baking powder
½ – ¾ cup (125–180 ml) cake flour
½ t (2.5 ml) salt
1 egg, beaten
salt and pepper
1 medium sweet pepper, deseeded
    and chopped
1 small red chilli, thinly sliced
1 T (15 ml) olive oil
1 medium avocado, sliced
juice of 2 limes
handful of fresh coriander

1. Cook the chunks of sweet potato in a pot of boiling water until soft. Drain and mash with the oil until smooth.
2. Whisk in the milk and ginger and leave to cool.
3. Sieve the dry ingredients together and stir into the sweet potato along with the beaten egg until smooth. Season to taste.
4. Cook the pepper and chilli in the olive oil until soft. Season to taste and set aside.
5. Fry spoonfuls of the sweet potato batter in a little hot oil in a non-stick frying pan until golden brown on both sides. Serve topped with slices of avocado, some sautéed peppers, a squeeze of lime juice and coriander garnish.

Serves 4

BLING-BLING BABA GHANOUSH

Place a plate of this sexy aubergine (eggplant) dip in front of me as tapas for drinks and I'll eat from the palm of your hand. - Jade

BABA GHANOUSH

2 medium aubergines, sliced into
    thick rounds
¼ cup (60 ml) olive oil
½ cup (125 ml) plain yoghurt
juice of 1 lemon
¼ cup (60 ml) tahini
2 T (30 ml) chopped fresh mint
salt and pepper

4 medium potatoes, peeled and very
    thinly sliced
¼ cup (60 ml) olive oil
salt and pepper
125 g fresh pomegranate rubies, crushed

1. Preheat the oven to 200 ºC.
2. Place the aubergine rounds on a baking tray, drizzle over the olive oil and roast for 30 minutes until soft.
3. Toss the potato slices in the second amount of olive oil on a baking tray, season well and bake for 25 minutes until golden brown and crispy. Remove from the oven and set aside to cool.
4. Blend all the ingredients for the baba ghanoush in a food processor, adding more olive oil if needed. Transfer to a serving plate and sprinkle over the crushed pomegranate rubies, letting the juices soak in.
5. Stick the potato crisps into the ghanoush and serve.

COOK'S TIP: Traditionally the aubergines are grilled on top of a gas stove, but I find this way works just as well.

Serves 4-6

SUNBURST FRUIT PLATTER WITH HONEY-NUT RICOTTA

2 ripe honeydew melons, peeled,
    deseeded and cut into wedges
1 large bunch seedless grapes, rinsed
2 medium pineapples, peeled and cut
    into wedges
8 fresh figs, halved
2 mangoes or nectarines, peeled and cut
    into chunks
2 starfruit or kiwi fruit, peeled and
    thinly sliced
250–300 g ricotta (see page 182)
3 T (45 ml) mascarpone
¼ cup (60 ml) organic honey
1 T (15 ml) chopped preserved
    ginger (optional)
½ cup (125 ml) fresh organic nuts,
    any kind
grated zest of 1 small lime or lemon
pinch of ground cinnamon
handful of fresh mint leaves
handful of pomegranate rubies
chilled lime wedges to serve

1. Arrange the fruits in a pretty sunburst pattern on a large serving plate.
2. Mix the ricotta and mascarpone with the honey, ginger (if using) and nuts. Spoon into a ramekin and upturn at the base of the sunburst.
3. Scatter over the grated zest, cinnamon, mint leaves and pomegranate rubies. Serve chilled with lime wedges.

Serve 8

BREAKFAST ANTIPASTI PLATTER

Great for entertaining, big on visual appeal and child's play to assemble. Raid the deli shelves for this one, to make the most of jars of pickled relishes. Bocconcini are little fresh mozzarella balls available from most good supermarkets and delis. If you can't find them, use 3 cm cubes top-quality mozzarella instead. Holiday food par excellence! Choose from any of the following ingredients:

16 pickled or freshly boiled and shelled
    quails' eggs, halved
10–14 labneh (see page 184) or goat's
    cheese balls rolled in dukkah
    (see page 177)
1 x 210 g pickled mushrooms, drained
8 marinated artichokes, quartered
8 figs, quartered
1 cup (250 ml) sundried tomatoes in oil,
    drained and snipped in half
large handful of mixed olives
large handful of rocket leaves
110 g readymade croutons

CRUMBED BOCCONCINI

400 g bocconcini balls or ordinary
    mozzarella cut into 3 cm cubes
$^2/_3$ cup (160 ml) cake flour
3 eggs, beaten
1 cup (250 ml) breadcrumbs
sunflower oil for frying

1. To make the crumbed bocconcini, roll the mozzarella balls or cubes first in the flour, then the beaten egg and finally coat in breadcrumbs. Repeat two more times for a thorough crumb 'jacket'. Set in a single layer on a plate and refrigerate until needed.
2. Fry 4 or 5 mozzarella balls at a time in hot shallow oil until just golden brown on all sides – not more than 2 minutes. Remove with a slotted spoon and drain briefly on absorbent paper towel.
3. To assemble the platter, arrange all the ingredients attractively on a large serving platter and dish up.

Serves 8

BAKED SPICED APPLES WITH SULTANAS, HONEY AND GREEK YOGHURT

This recipe is easy to double up for larger numbers. Baking apples like Bramleys are hard to find these days, so I use Golden Delicious or Red Gala. An apple corer will help you core the apples neatly for the filling. - Sonia

4 large apples, washed and cored
2 cups (500 ml) Greek or vanilla
    yoghurt, chilled
pinch of ground cinnamon

FILLING
100 g pecan nuts, coarsely chopped
½ t (2.5 ml) ground cinnamon
¼ t (1 ml) ground nutmeg
¼ cup (60 ml) soft brown sugar
¼ cup (60 ml) golden sultanas
2 T (30 ml) unsalted butter or margarine
½ t (2.5 ml) almond essence

SYRUP
5 T (75 ml) honey
1 cup (250 ml) water
¼ t (1 ml) ground ginger
3 T (45 ml) brandy

1. Preheat the oven to 180 °C.
2. Pack the apples closely together in a baking dish just big enough to hold them all snugly.
3. Mix all the filling ingredients together and stuff into the cavities of the apples.
4. To make the syrup, bring the honey and water to the boil and boil for 2 minutes before removing from the heat. Stir in the ginger and brandy and pour around the apples.
5. Bake for 45–60 minutes until the apples are completely soft when a toothpick is inserted. Serve hot or cold with Greek yoghurt and a dusting of cinnamon.

Serves 4

CHOCOLATE AND CINNAMON PANCAKES WITH ORANGE BUTTER

Pancakes freeze very well if stored between sheets of wax paper and the whole stack wrapped in clingfilm. Use a good chocolate spread to make this glam pudding in next to no time. Make the orange butter ahead of time too and refrigerate, rolled up in clingfilm. This has been adapted from a Donna Hay recipe.

12 pancakes (see page 173)
2 T (30 ml) mascarpone
1 cup (250 ml) chocolate spread
    or 1¼ cup (125 g) grated
    dark chocolate
½ cup (125 ml) melted butter
1 cup (250 ml) cold pouring cream

CINNAMON SUGAR
½ cup (125 ml) castor sugar
1 t (5 ml) ground cinnamon

ORANGE BUTTER
3 T (45 ml) Seville marmalade
grated zest of ½ orange
½ cup (125 ml) unsalted butter, softened

1. First make the pancakes.
2. To make the orange butter, mash the marmalade and orange zest into the butter until very well blended. Form into a log, roll up in clingfilm and refrigerate until needed.
3. Mix the castor sugar and cinnamon and spread evenly on a plate.
4. Mix the mascarpone and chocolate spread or grated chocolate together.
5. Spread one side of each pancake with the chocolate filling and fold over in half, and over again to form triangles.
6. Brush each side of the pancake triangles with melted butter and press into the cinnamon sugar. Set aside on a plate.
7. Heat the remaining melted butter in a small non-stick frying pan and fry each pancake on both sides until the cinnamon sugar caramelises. Arrange the pancakes in a dish and dot with orange butter. Let the butter melt and serve with cold pouring cream.

Serves 4-6

Deluxe Dinner

PESTO PUFF PASTRY PALMIERS

Palmiers are little puff pastry rolls usually served sweet, but are equally delicious as a savoury titbit when made with pesto, tapenade, plain grated Parmesan or even some chermoula spread on the pastry before baking. Serve warm from the oven with drinks before dinner.

1 x 400 g roll frozen puff pastry, thawed
    in the fridge overnight
½ cup (125 ml) basil pesto

1. Roll out the pastry and spread with the pesto.
2. Roll up one side of the pastry until you reach the middle, then repeat with the other side. Place the roll on a baking tray and freeze for 30 minutes.
3. Preheat the oven to 200 °C. Lightly spray two baking trays with non-stick cooking spray and line with wax paper.
4. When ready to bake, slice the roll into 1 cm-thick slices and lay them next to each other on the baking trays, leaving 3 cm in between each.
5. Bake for 15–20 minutes until puffed up and golden brown. Serve warm or at room temperature.

Makes 20

THAI PUMPKIN SOUP

1.5 kg pumpkin or butternut, peeled
    and cut into chunks
1 medium onion, peeled and
    finely chopped
1 stalk lemongrass, tender inner part
    only, finely minced
1 T (15 ml) grated fresh ginger
1 T (15 ml) sunflower oil
1 t (5 ml) sesame oil
¼ cup (60 ml) Thai red curry paste
1 x 420 g can low-fat coconut milk,
    reserve 2 T (30 ml)
3½ cups (875 ml) vegetable stock
1 T (15 ml) fresh lime juice
grated zest of 1 lime
3 T (45 ml) each of chopped fresh
    coriander and mint
1 small red chilli, thinly sliced

1. Preheat the oven to 200 °C and roast the pumpkin or butternut chunks on a baking tray for 20 minutes until aromatic and tender.
2. Meanwhile, cook the onion, lemongrass and ginger in the oils in a large pot until the onion is soft and translucent.
3. Add the pumpkin/butternut, curry paste, coconut milk, vegetable stock and lime juice and cook over medium heat until very tender. Use a stick blender to liquidise the soup until very smooth.
4. Garnish with the lime zest, herbs, chilli and reserved coconut milk and serve piping hot.

Serves 6

POTATO SOUFFLÉS WITH LEMON ASPARAGUS

Soufflés aren't difficult to make at all, just serve them immediately while still gorgeously puffed up. Steam fresh asparagus spears first, dress with lemon olive oil and set aside for serving. Make the white sauce base for the soufflés up to 4 hours ahead, leaving the egg whites to be beaten at the last minute. If making ahead, brush the surface of the white sauce with a little melted butter and lay a sheet of clingfilm over it to prevent a 'skin' from forming.

2 T (30 ml) breadcrumbs or
    grated Parmesan
1 kg floury potatoes, peeled and cut
    into chunks
6 T (90 ml) butter
celery salt and pepper
¼ t (1 ml) cayenne pepper
¼ t (1 ml) mustard powder
¼ cup (60 ml) butter
1 cup (250 ml) warm milk
¼ cup (60 ml) cake flour
2 t (10 ml) baking powder
3 egg yolks
1 cup (250 ml) grated Gruyère
    or Parmesan
6 egg whites
pinch of salt

1. Preheat the oven to 200 °C.
2. Spray four 1¼ cup-capacity soufflé ramekins with non-stick cooking spray and stand on a baking tray, a few centimetres apart, until needed. Dust the inside of each ramekin with the breadcrumbs or grated Parmesan.
3. Cook the potatoes in salted boiling water until soft. Drain and mash thoroughly, then mash in the first amount of butter and seasonings up to and including the mustard powder.
4. To make soufflé base, melt the second amount of butter in the warm milk in a saucepan over low heat. Sift in the dry ingredients and whisk until smooth. Cook the white sauce over gentle heat for 5 minutes, stirring constantly to prevent the bottom scorching.
5. When the sauce is thick, remove from the heat and mix well in a bowl with the mashed potato, egg yolks and Gruyère or Parmesan. Stir until smooth.
6. Beat the egg whites with a pinch of salt until very stiff and, using a large metal spoon, gently fold through the soufflé until no white streaks can be seen. Work gently so as not to lose the air trapped in the egg whites, as this will cause the soufflés to fall flat.
7. Spoon the mixture into the ramekins and place the baking tray in the middle of the oven. Bake for 25–30 minutes until puffy and golden brown, and the centres have set. Serve immediately with lemon asparagus (see recipe intro).

Serves 4-6

CARBONADA CRIOLLA

Whole, stuffed, baked pumpkin with sweet potato, sweetcorn, tomatoes and peaches. I served this at my South American-themed 30th birthday party in London - it's as delicious as it is spectacular to look at. Serve with the beautiful jewelled burghul on page 108. Just make sure the pumpkin you buy fits inside your oven! For a really large feast you could bake a variety of different kinds and sizes of squashes. - Sonia

4–6 kg whole, unblemished pumpkin
3 T (45 ml) olive oil
2 t (10 ml) sugar

FILLING
3 medium onions, peeled and chopped
    into chunks
1 T (15 ml) crushed fresh garlic
3 large very ripe tomatoes, peeled and
    chopped into chunks
2 large sweet peppers, deseeded and
    chopped into chunks
3 bay leaves
2 t (10 ml) fresh origanum or
    1 t (5 ml) dried
salt and pepper
oil for frying
1 kg sweet potato, peeled and cut
    into chunks
1 kg Mediterranean potatoes, peeled and
    cut into thick slices
2 T (30 ml) tomato purée
4 cups (1 litre) vegetable stock
1 cup (250 ml) dried peaches or apricots,
    roughly chopped
1 cup (250 ml) dried pears or apple rings,
    roughly chopped
300 g mixed courgettes and patty pans,
    thickly sliced
3 fresh sweetcorn cobs, cleaned and
    sliced 3 cm thick
handful of fresh coriander
2 medium red chillies, sliced
¼ cup (60 ml) sour cream (optional)

1. Preheat the oven to 180 °C.
2. Scrub the pumpkin very well under running water. Using a very sharp knife, carefully slice off a lid from the top of the pumpkin, leaving the stem on to use as a handle. Set aside. Use a metal spoon to scoop out the fibrous pulp and pips inside, leaving a sturdy rim that won't collapse once the pumpkin is baked.
3. Use absorbent paper towel to blot the inside of the pumpkin dry, then brush the outside with the olive oil and sprinkle evenly with the sugar. Put on a baking tray and bake for 1 hour. The pumpkin should be firm but tender when pierced with a toothpick.
4. To make the filling, cook the onions, garlic, tomatoes, peppers, herbs and seasoning in oil in a large saucepan over medium heat for 15 minutes.
5. Add the sweet and Mediterranean potato chunks, tomato purée and stock. Cook for 30 minutes until tender.
6. Add the dried fruit, courgettes and sweetcorn, check for seasoning and cook for a further 10 minutes.
7. Spoon the mixture into the pumpkin shell and bake for 20 minutes until warmed through. Garnish with coriander, chilli and sour cream if desired.

Serves 6-8

WILD MUSHROOM LASAGNE

Use any mushrooms you can find, including rehydrated dried ones.
Just remember to strain the soaking water to go into to the sauce, and
rinse rehydrated mushrooms well under running water to remove any grit.
A comforting yet luxurious main course.

SAUCE

3 cups (750 ml) warm milk
2 T (30 ml) butter
2 T (30 ml) cake flour
¼ t (1 ml) grated nutmeg

FILLING

2 bay leaves
1 large onion, peeled and finely chopped
2 t (10 ml) crushed fresh garlic
3 T (45 ml) butter
1 T (15 ml) olive oil
1 kg mixed mushrooms, wiped clean and
    thickly sliced
1 T (15 ml) chopped fresh thyme
    or rosemary
1 cup (250 ml) mushroom or
    vegetable stock
1 T (15 ml) tomato concentrate
salt and pepper
500 g instant dried lasagne sheets
300 g Fontina, Gruyère or mozzarella
    cheese, grated
½ cup (125 ml) grated Parmesan

1. First make the sauce by heating the milk and butter together in a saucepan until the butter has melted, then sift over the flour and nutmeg, and whisk furiously until completely smooth.
2. Turn down the heat and let the sauce simmer with barely a bubble for about 10 minutes until nicely thickened. Stir constantly to prevent scorching.
3. Preheat the oven to 180 °C.
4. Cook the bay leaves, onion and garlic in the butter and olive oil in a pot for about 5 minutes until the onion is soft and translucent.
5. Add the mushrooms, including any drained soaked ones, and herbs, turn up the heat and cook while stirring until all the moisture has evaporated.
6. Add the stock and tomato concentrate and turn down the heat to simmer. Cook until the sauce is thickened and season well. Remove the bay leaves.
7. Lightly oil the base of an ovenproof dish and line with instant lasagne sheets. Spread over a quarter of the white sauce, then follow with a third of the mushroom mixture and then a third of the grated Fontina, Gruyère or mozzarella (not the Parmesan). Repeat with lasagne, sauce, mushrooms and cheese until you finally end with a layer of lasagne.
8. Cover with the remaining white sauce, sprinkle over the Parmesan and bake in the middle of the oven for 45–55 minutes, until golden brown and the sauce is bubbling. It might be wise to place a baking tray underneath the lasagne dish to catch any drips.
9. Keep warm until ready to serve.

Serve 8

JEWELLED BURGHUL

This makes a glorious multi-coloured centrepiece for a festive table. Without the fresh herbs, the burghul will last three days in the refrigerator, so it's perfect for holiday entertaining.

2 cups (500 ml) boiling water
2 t (10 ml) vegetable stock powder
1 t (5 ml) crushed cardamom seeds
½ t (2.5 ml) ground cinnamon
3 T (45 ml) lemon or lime juice
2 cups (500 ml) burghul,
    thoroughly rinsed
1 cup (250 ml) golden sultanas
1 cup (250 ml) shelled pistachios
1 cup (250 ml) pomegranate rubies or
    dried cranberries
½ cup (125 ml) pumpkin seeds, toasted
¼ cup (60 ml) extra-virgin olive oil
3 T (45 ml) each of chopped fresh dill,
    coriander, mint and parsley
salt and pepper

1. Mix the boiling water with the vegetable stock powder, cardamom, cinnamon and lemon or lime juice, and pour over the rinsed burghul in a large bowl. Leave to stand for 30–45 minutes and then squeeze out all the excess liquid between your hands to drain.
2. Place the drained burghul in a large bowl and fork through the remaining ingredients. Season well, and chill or serve at room temperature. Burghul will retain a slightly chewy texture, unlike couscous which can become very mushy.

Serves 8

Imam bayildi

This slow-baked aubergine (eggplant) with tomato and olive oil is a legendary Turkish dish meaning 'the Imam fainted'.

3 T (45 ml) olive oil, plus extra
    for drizzling
2 onions, peeled and thinly sliced
1 x 410 g can chopped peeled tomatoes
2 t (10 ml) crushed fresh garlic
3 T (45 ml) chopped fresh parsley
2 t (10 ml) sugar
pinch of ground cardamom
pinch of ground coriander
salt and pepper
4 medium aubergines
juice of ½ lemon
Greek yoghurt to serve

1. Preheat the oven to 180 °C. Pour 2 T (30 ml) of the olive oil into a baking dish large enough to hold the aubergines and filling.
2. Fry the onions in the remaining oil in a saucepan over medium heat for 6–7 minutes until soft and translucent.
3. Add the tomatoes, garlic, parsley, sugar, spices and seasoning and cook for a further 5 minutes, until reasonably thick (not watery).
4. Starting 2 cm from the stem ends, cut three slits into each aubergine and fan out slightly.
5. Put the aubergines in the baking dish. Hold the slits apart and spoon some of the tomato-onion mixture between each.
6. Drizzle over the lemon juice and a little olive oil, season well, cover with foil and bake for 40 minutes or until tender. Remove the foil and bake for a further 10 minutes to give it some colour. Serve hot or cold with yoghurt.

Serves 4

Buffalo mozzarella with orange crème fraîche and thyme

I love surprising people with this instead of a humdrum cheese platter. - Jade

juice and zest of 1 orange
250 g crème fraîche
1 t (5 ml) sea-salt flakes
freshly ground black pepper
4 x 125 g balls buffalo mozzarella
4–6 T (60–90 ml) pomegranate rubies
2 t (10 ml) chopped fresh lemon
    thyme leaves
olive oil for drizzling

1. Mix the orange juice and half of the zest with the crème fraîche, salt and pepper. Refrigerate for 30 minutes.
2. Break the mozzarella balls in half, arrange on a serving platter and spoon over the orange crème fraîche.
3. Sprinkle over the remaining orange zest, as well as the pomegranate rubies and lemon thyme. Grind over more black pepper and finish by drizzling over a little olive oil. Serve at room temperature or slightly chilled with some crusty sourdough bread.

Serves 4

SAFFRON RICE PILAFF WITH ALMONDS AND MINTED YOGHURT

Making a true Persian rice pilaff is considered an art: somewhat laborious, but well worth the extra effort. Usually served only at very special occasions, it may include dried fruit, nuts, herbs and exotic spices. Saffron provides the luscious golden hues.

500 g basmati rice

20 threads saffron

1 cup (250 ml) plain yoghurt

12 mint leaves, torn

1 cup (250 ml) diced butternut, tossed in olive oil

salt and pepper

6 cardamom pods

3 T (45 ml) unsalted butter or ghee

2 T (30 ml) each of finely chopped fresh mint, coriander, parsley and chives

½ cup (125 ml) sultanas (optional)

½ cup (125 ml) flaked almonds, lightly toasted

1. Rinse the rice in a sieve under running water until the water runs completely clear. Place the rice in a bowl, cover completely with cold water and leave to stand for 2 hours.
2. Preheat the oven to 180 °C.
3. Pour 2 T (30 ml) boiling water over the saffron threads in a small bowl and soak for 10 minutes, before crushing with the back of a spoon to release colour and flavour.
4. Mix the yoghurt with the mint and set aside.
5. Roast the oil-coated butternut cubes on a baking tray for about 25 minutes until just tender. Season lightly and set aside.
6. Meanwhile, fill a large heavy-based pot three-quarters full with salted water, put on the lid and bring to the boil. Drain the rice from its soaking water and pour into the pot of rapidly boiling water. Add the cardamom pods. Cook for 2 minutes exactly, and then strain through a sieve. Rinse the rice very well under running warm water to remove starch.
7. Wipe the inside of the pot dry, heat the butter or ghee to almost smoking point and add half of the pre-cooked, rinsed rice.
8. Cover the rice with the butternut, herbs and sultanas if using, top with the remaining rice and pour over the saffron water. Cover the pot with a double-thick layer of foil as well as the lid.
9. Turn the heat to minimum, and cook gently for 35 minutes. Remove the pot from the heat, keeping it covered.
10. Set the pot-base in a sink filled with a little cold water and leave it for 2 minutes. This loosens the crust that has formed on the bottom of the pot. The crust is highly prized as the best part of the pilaff.
11. Now remove the lid and foil and use a fork to fluff up the rice, and fork through the almonds. Serve with the minted yoghurt on the side.

Serves 4

GRILLED LEEK, ASPARAGUS AND GREEN BEAN SALAD WITH BLACK OLIVE AND LEMON DRESSING

If you have a barbecue going, grill the baby leeks over the coals, otherwise use a stove-top griddle pan. Roasting under an oven grill won't do any harm either. Buy jars of black olive paste or tapenade from any good deli or supermarket if you're not up to making tapenade yourself.

500 g baby leeks, washed and trimmed of
    roots and green stalk ends
200 g fine asparagus
2 T (30 ml) olive oil
salt
300 g fine green beans, rinsed, topped
    and tailed

DRESSING
½ cup (125 ml) black olives, pitted
1 t (5 ml) crushed fresh garlic
1 t (5 ml) capers, rinsed and
    chopped finely
½ t (2.5 ml) chilli flakes (optional)
1 T (15 ml) brandy (optional)
4–5 T (60–75 ml) olive oil
1 T (15 ml) finely chopped fresh thyme
    or parsley
grated zest of 1 lemon

1. Brush the leeks and asparagus lightly with olive oil, season with salt and grill on all sides until lightly charred.
2. Cook the beans for 3 minutes in a large pot of rapidly boiling salted water. Drain and cool.
3. Mix all the ingredients for the dressing, crush finely with a pestle and mortar or in a food processor and toss through the cooled vegetables to serve.

Serves 6

4-TOMATO SALAD WITH BUFFALO MOZZARELLA AND BASIL OIL

Vegans, omit the mozzarella.

4 large, very ripe beefsteak tomatoes,
    plunged into boiling water for
    45 seconds to peel
1 cup (250 ml) sundried tomatoes in oil
200 g ripe Rosa tomatoes, halved
120 g yellow plum tomatoes or vine
    tomatoes, halved
¼ cup (60 ml) basil oil (see page 181)
2 T (30 ml) balsamic vinegar
salt and pepper
1 x 125 g ball buffalo mozzarella

1. When ready to assemble the salad, peel the large tomatoes, slice vertically into eighths to form petals and cut away the seeds. Chill until needed.
2. Drain the oil off the sundried tomatoes and reserve. Snip the sundried tomatoes in half and add to the chilled tomato petals.
3. Add the Rosa and yellow plum or vine tomatoes.
4. Add the reserved sundried tomato oil to ¼ cup (60 ml) of the basil oil. Mix well and drizzle over the salad, add a splash of balsamic vinegar and season well.
5. Tear chunks off the mozzarella ball and scatter over the salad. Serve within 3 hours of making.

Serves 6

SAVOURY PANCAKE STACK WITH PORCINI MUSHROOMS, TOMATO AND PARMESAN

If you've been clever enough to make and freeze pancakes from the recipe in Basics, as well as some basic tomato sauce, this recipe is a breeze and will stand for hours before being baked to serve. Rehydrate dried porcini or use fresh. Garnish with a peppery rocket leaves drizzled with fruity olive oil, balsamic vinegar and a few drops of truffle oil.

12 medium (about 22 cm diameter) pancakes
2 cups (500 ml) rich tomato sauce (see page 184)
2 cups (500 ml) cooked sliced porcini or portabellini mushrooms
Handful of parsley, finely chopped
½ cup (125 ml) chopped chives
1 cup (250 ml) each grated Gruyère, Parmesan and mozzarella

WHITE SAUCE
1½ cups (375 ml) milk
2T (30 ml) butter
2T (30 ml) flour
Salt and pepper
Pinch of grated nutmeg

1. Preheat oven to 180 °C.
2. Make the white sauce by bringing the milk and butter to the boil, then whisking in the flour until smooth. Turn heat down very low and cook gently while stirring for about 12 minutes, until thick.
3. Stir in the tomato sauce, mushrooms and herbs and season to taste.
4. Toss the Gruyère and Parmesan cheese together, keeping the mozzarella separate.
5. Layer the pancakes with the sauce and cheeses in a greased baking dish, starting with a layer of tomato sauce. Finish with tomato/mushroom sauce, the Gruyère and Parmesan mix, mozzarella, salt and pepper. Cover with foil and bake for 20 minutes, then remove foil and let brown for another 12 minutes. Serve hot in thin wedges as it's very filling.

Serves 6 - 8

WHITE CHOCOLATE MOUSSE
WITH CHILLI GRILLED PINEAPPLE

I savoured a chunk of pineapple seasoned with chilli salt at a Johannesburg market one day and promptly devised this dish around it. Chilli pineapple pairs with the sexy, creamy mousse to round off a dinner or braai in grand style. - Jade

200 g white chocolate, chopped
200 ml cream
4 egg whites
2 T (30 ml) castor sugar, plus 1 T (15 ml)
    extra for dusting
4 wedges pineapple
1 T (15 ml) chilli salt (see below)

1. Melt the white chocolate in a double-boiler over low heat. Leave to cool slightly.
2. Bring the cream to the boil in a saucepan and turn off the heat.
3. Whisk the egg whites to form stiff peaks, whisking in the castor sugar towards the end.
4. Pour about a third of the cream into the chocolate, whisking in well to blend, before following with the remaining cream.
5. Use a metal spoon to fold one large spoonful of beaten egg white into the chocolate and cream mixture, and then gently fold in the remaining egg white. Make sure no white streaks show. Work gently so as not to lose any volume.
6. Spoon into pots or coffee cups, put on a tray and refrigerate until firm, at least 3 hours or overnight.
7. When ready to serve, preheat the oven's grill or use the stove-top grill pan. About 15 minutes before serving, sprinkle the extra castor sugar over the pineapple, and pop under the grill or on the pan for 30 seconds on each side to caramelise. Remove from the heat and sprinkle over some chilli salt.
8. Serve the pineapple to dip into the cold white chocolate mousse.

Serves 4

CHILLI SALT

3 T (45 ml) sea-salt flakes
1 t (5 ml) dried chilli powder
1 t (5 ml) paprika
½ t (2.5 ml) cayenne pepper
2 T (30 ml) castor sugar

1. Grind all the ingredients together in a mortar and pestle to blend the mixture and release the flavours. Use immediately or store in an airtight container.

Makes about 6 T (90 ml)

MINI PAVLOVAS WITH GRANADILLA CREAM
AND RASPBERRY CURD

Meringues are very impressive desserts, easily made in advance and stored in airtight containers. Just don't try to bake them on humid days. As a child an ice cream and caramel pavlova was my favourite birthday treat. The curd niftily uses some of the egg yolks left after whipping the egg whites for the meringues. Start the day before you wish to serve the pavlovas. - Sonia

MERINGUES

4 egg whites
pinch of salt
240 g castor sugar
½ T (7.5 ml) cornflour
1 t (5 ml) white wine vinegar
½ t (2.5 ml) vanilla essence

RASPBERRY CURD

3 egg yolks
juice and zest of 1 lime
30 g unsalted butter
40 g castor sugar
200 g raspberries, liquidised and forced
    through a strainer to remove pips

GRANADILLA CREAM

300 ml cream
¼ cup (60 ml) icing sugar
¼ cup (60 ml) granadilla pulp

4 small ripe bananas, thinly sliced on
    the diagonal
½ cup (125 ml) fresh raspberries
½ cup (125 ml) flaked almonds, toasted
icing sugar for dusting

1. Preheat the oven to 150 °C. Grease two baking trays and line them with baking paper.
2. Whisk the egg whites until stiff peaks form. While whisking, gradually add the salt, castor sugar and cornflour and carry on whisking until the egg whites are very stiff and glossy.
3. Fold in the vinegar and vanilla essence with a large metal spoon, being careful not to lose any of the volume.
4. Drop 4–6 large mounds of meringue onto the prepared baking trays or make two circular or rectangular shapes. Make the edges of the meringues slightly higher than the centres.
5. Bake for 30 minutes in the middle of the oven. Then, without ever opening the oven door, switch off the oven and leave the meringues inside for a further 30 minutes.
6. Remove and cool on a wire rack before storing in airtight containers.
7. To make the raspberry curd, whisk all the ingredients together in a metal bowl. Place the bowl over a pot of gently simmering water, making sure the bottom of the bowl doesn't touch the water. Keep on whisking gently for 15–20 minutes until the mixture thickens and begins to pull away from the sides of the bowl. Set aside and leave to cool before storing in an airtight container.
8. To make the granadilla cream, beat the cream until very thick and stiff peaks form. Whisk in the icing sugar and granadilla pulp and refrigerate until needed.
9. To serve, spread the raspberry curd over each pavlova or in the middle of a large one. Cover with thin diagonal slices of banana and fresh raspberries, and spoon over dollops of granadilla cream. Sprinkle over toasted flaked almonds, dust with icing sugar, and serve. This is best assembled no more than 20 minutes before serving.

Serves 4-6

CHURROS AND
REAL HOT CHOCOLATE

Relax

SOUL FOOD FOR SLOW DAYS

CHURROS

I ate churros for breakfast for the first time in Barcelona and instantly fell in love with all things Spanish. Eat churros as soon as you make them - they are perfect rainy day food. Use a piping bag to squeeze the batter into the hot oil. Dust with cinnamon sugar as soon as the churros have drained on absorbent paper towel. Serve with real hot chocolate (see opposite). - Sonia

½ cup (125 ml) castor sugar
1 T (15 ml) ground cinnamon
150 ml water
50 g unsalted butter
2 T (30 ml) castor sugar
1 cup (250 ml) cake flour
¼ t (1 ml) salt
2 large eggs, well beaten
3 cups (750 ml) sunflower oil

1. Mix the castor sugar and cinnamon and spread on a plate.
2. Bring the water, butter and castor sugar to the boil in a small saucepan.
3. Tip the flour and salt in all at once and stir furiously with a wooden spoon to blend.
4. Immediately draw the saucepan off the heat and continue to beat with the wooden spoon for about 30 seconds, until the dough pulls away from the sides of the pan and forms a ball.
5. Let the dough stand for 5–7 minutes to cool slightly, then start beating in the eggs a tablespoon at a time, beating energetically to make sure every little bit of egg is incorporated before you add more. This is the hard part of making churros!
6. Once you have accomplished that, cover the bowl and refrigerate for at least 20 minutes.
7. To cook, heat the sunflower oil in a large, deep saucepan. The oil should not take up more than a third of the pan.
8. Spoon the churros batter into a piping bag. Test the heat of the oil: once a little dot of the batter bubbles up to the surface straightaway and starts turning colour, it's ready.
9. Pipe three 7–9 cm lengths of batter at a time into the oil, keeping them separate. Use two forks to turn them in the oil, making sure they cook golden brown on all sides, about 2 minutes.
10. Use a slotted spoon to remove the churros. Drain on absorbent paper towel, roll in cinnamon sugar and serve warm.

Makes 12

REAL HOT CHOCOLATE

I like using Honest Chocolate's organic dairy-free chocolate spread for this, but make sure you use chocolate with at least 70% cocoa solids. Rice, almond and soy milk make perfect dairy substitutes. - Sonia

4 cups (1 litre) full-cream milk

1 vanilla pod, split and seeds scraped
    into milk

150 g plain milk or dark chocolate, broken
    into pieces

1–2 T (15–30 ml) dark brown sugar

1 T (15 ml) very finely grated chocolate

1. Bring the milk, vanilla pod and seeds to the boil in a saucepan. Add the chocolate pieces and sugar and remove from the heat when the chocolate has melted.
2. Whisk until frothy and pour into warmed mugs. Dust with grated chocolate and serve hot.

COOK'S TIP: Warm mugs by filling briefly with boiling water before emptying again.

Serves 4

VEGAN FRENCH TOAST WITH BANANA AND HONEY

I made this Sunday breakfast treat for my vegan sister and it's been a winner ever since. - Jade

4 bananas

1½ cups (375 ml) soy milk

1 t (5 ml) ground cinnamon

1 t (5 ml) vanilla essence

8 slices thick-cut white bread or
    French loaf

sunflower oil for frying

honey for drizzling

fresh berries to serve

1. Liquidise or blend the bananas with the milk, cinnamon and vanilla essence in a food processor or using a stick blender.
2. Dip the bread slices into the mixture just to coat both sides, not to soak.
3. Heat oil in a frying pan over medium heat and fry the slices for 1 minute on each side until golden brown. Serve drizzled with honey and topped with fresh berries.

Serves 4

RICOTTA PANCAKES WITH BERRIES AND HONEYCOMB MASCARPONE

An indulgence for lazy days. Serve with berries or caramelised apple or make savoury versions as given in the Cook's tip below. Alternatively, I like to add 3 T (45 ml) thinly sliced soft dried apricots to the batter. - Sonia

¼ cup (60 ml) castor sugar
100 g cake flour
pinch of salt
1 t (5 ml) baking powder
250 g ricotta (see page 182)
3 large eggs, separated
¼ cup (60 ml) oil
¼ cup (60 ml) organic honeycomb
½ cup (125 ml) mascarpone
1½ cups (375 ml) fresh berries
pinch of ground cinnamon

1. Sift together the dry ingredients.
2. Beat the ricotta, egg yolks and 1 T (15 ml) of the oil together until smooth. Fold into the dry ingredients.
3. Whisk the egg whites until very stiff and fold into the batter with a large metal spoon, working carefully to retain as much volume as possible.
4. Heat a large non-stick frying pan and pour 1 T (15 ml) of the oil into it.
5. Drop heaped tablespoons of batter into the hot pan and cook over medium heat on both sides until golden brown. Remove and keep warm while you use up all the batter. Re-oil the pan as needed.
6. Mash the honeycomb into the mascarpone.
7. Serve the pancakes hot topped with berries, some honeycomb mascarpone and a pinch of cinnamon.

COOK'S TIP: Make savoury pancakes by omitting the sugar and adding chopped herbs, grated Parmesan or blue cheese or 4 very finely sliced sundried tomatoes. Serve with grilled mushrooms and avocado salsa.

Serves 4

SONIA'S GYPSY EGGS

Beautifully golden egg yolks melting into a hot, rich tomato sauce, with a dollop of cold spiced yoghurt and some toasted pitas make a comforting meal any time of the day. Sumac is a deep red, lemony and slightly tart spice ground from sumac berries and is very popular in the Middle East as a seasoning for salads, hummus, rice pilaffs and onion salads.

1 small leek, rinsed and sliced
1 small fennel bulb, thinly sliced
3 T (45 ml) olive oil
1 t (5 ml) smoked paprika
1 x 410 g can chickpeas or white
    cannellini beans, rinsed under
    running water
1 x 410 g can plum or chopped tomatoes
    in juice
2 large handfuls (about 50 g) of baby
    spinach, rinsed, dried and torn
salt and pepper
4 large eggs

SPICED YOGHURT

1 t (5 ml) crushed fresh garlic (optional)
salt and pepper
2 T (30 ml) extra-virgin olive oil
1 cup (250 ml) creamy Greek yoghurt
1 t (5 ml) sumac powder

1. Cook the leek and fennel in the olive oil in a large frying pan for 8–10 minutes until very soft and translucent.
2. Add the smoked paprika, chickpeas or beans and tomatoes and cook for another 10 minutes until thickened. Stir through the torn spinach leaves until wilted. Season well.
3. Use the back of a spoon to make four hollows in the sauce. Break an egg carefully into each hollow and cover with a lid or plate. Cook for about 3 minutes or until the eggs are just set. Remove from the heat and dish up.
4. To make the spiced yoghurt, stir the garlic (if using), salt, pepper and olive oil through the yoghurt and spoon a dollop next to each gypsy egg. Sprinkle sumac over and serve immediately.

Serves 4

HOMEMADE CHAKALAKA WITH ROTIS

When a Xhosa mama and a Cape Malay auntie met, they had this for lunch. If you can find rotis made the traditional Malay way, you're in luck! They should contain no dairy products, and are thus vegan friendly. Don't skimp and buy chakalaka, make your own and store in the fridge for peckish moments.

1 onion, peeled and sliced

3 T (45 ml) oil

1 T (15 ml) strong curry powder

1–2 small red chillies, chopped

½ t (2.5 ml) paprika

1 t (5 ml) salt

2–3 t (10–15 ml) crushed fresh garlic

3 large carrots, peeled and
coarsely grated

1 each of green, yellow and red pepper,
deseeded and sliced 1 cm thick

200 g green beans, topped, tailed and
chopped or 1 cup (250 ml) peas

1 small cauliflower head, washed and
broken into florets

½ small green cabbage, chopped

½ cup (125 ml) chutney

3 T (45 ml) vinegar

salt and pepper

4–6 readymade rotis

1. Fry the onion in the oil in a large saucepan until soft and brown.
2. Add the curry powder, chillies, paprika, salt, garlic, carrots and peppers and cook uncovered for 10 minutes.
3. Add the beans or peas, cauliflower and cabbage, and cook for a further 5 minutes, stirring continuously.
4. Stir in the chutney, vinegar, salt and pepper and cook for a further 10 minutes until thickened. It's vital that the cabbage retains some crunch and texture.
5. Heat the rotis and serve with the chakalaka.

Serves 4

ROOT VEGETABLE ROSTI WITH POACHED EGG AND CREAMED SPINACH

Use different root vegetables as an interesting alternative to plain potato. I like to make small flat disks, almost like pancakes, with poached egg and creamed spinach on top. - Jade

2 potatoes, peeled and coarsely grated
1 sweet potato, peeled and
    coarsely grated
1 parsnip, peeled and coarsely grated
1 carrot, peeled and coarsely grated
1 onion, peeled and roughly chopped
1 t (5 ml) grated fresh ginger
1 T (15 ml) cake flour
5 eggs
salt and pepper
3 T (45 ml) oil
2 handfuls of baby spinach, rinsed, dried
    and stalks removed
2 T (30 ml) mascarpone
squeeze lemon juice

1. Bring a large saucepan of salted water to the boil for poaching the eggs.
2. Meanwhile, mix the grated vegetables, onion and ginger, roll up like a Christmas cracker in a clean tea towel and wring to remove all excess liquid.
3. Mix the vegetables with the flour and 1 egg, season well and set aside.
4. To cook the rosti, heat the oil in a frying pan and fry spoonfuls at a time until crispy and golden brown, about 4 minutes each side. You can also fill the entire base of the pan with rosti mix if you want to cook large ones.
5. Poach the remaining 4 eggs in the boiling water and remove with a slotted spoon, patting dry with absorbent paper towel. Wilt the spinach with the mascarpone and lemon juice and season well. Spoon some spinach on each rosti, top with an egg and serve hot.

Serves 4

CONGEE

Congee is a traditional Chinese breakfast dish of rice very slowly cooked in copious amounts of stock or water until the grains disintegrate completely to form a thick porridge-like soup. It's the ultimate cheap and cheerful comfort food, especially when you're feeling poorly or cold. Don't be put off by the list of ingredients for the toppings - use whatever you like, or none! The recipe is simplicity itself. My children and I love this for Sunday brunches. - Sonia

200 g short-grain rice (brown short-grain is also good)
1 small red onion, peeled and very finely chopped
1 T (15 ml) grated fresh ginger
2 t (10 ml) crushed fresh garlic
2 medium carrots, peeled and finely chopped
1 T (15 ml) sesame oil
2 dried shiitake mushrooms, soaked in hot water for 30 minutes, drained and sliced
10 cups (2.5 litres) vegetable stock
light soy sauce for drizzling

TOPPINGS (USE ANY, ALL OR NONE, WHATEVER PLEASES YOUR HEART)

½ cup (125 ml) roasted peanuts, chopped
3 T (45 ml) chopped fresh coriander
1 small red chilli, very finely chopped
2 T (30 ml) slivered pickled ginger
4 spring onions, very thinly sliced
2 heads pak choi, washed and chopped
3 T (45 ml) peeled and very finely sliced fresh ginger
2 T (30 ml) pickled turnip: peel and dice two turnips, cover in vinegar and add 1 t (5 ml) salt
1 cup (250 ml) frozen petits pois, thawed by pouring over 2 cups (500 ml) boiling water and allowing to stand for 15 minutes

1. Rinse the rice in a sieve under running water until the water runs completely clear. Remove any darkened bits or stones.
2. In a very large pot, at least 8 litre capacity, sweat the onion, ginger, garlic and carrots in the sesame oil for 10 minutes. Add the shiitake mushrooms, rice and stock and bring to the boil.
3. As soon as it boils, turn down the heat to low and simmer gently for 1¾–2 hours, until the rice grains have broken down completely and the soup has a thick, porridge-like consistency. Stir from time to time to prevent the bottom scorching.
4. Drizzle with a little soy sauce and serve in bowls with a selection of toppings in little dishes for everyone to help themselves.

Serves 4-6

GREEK YOGHURT AND HERB PIE BAKED IN VINE LEAVES

When I'm in a hurry, I often simply wrap whole rounds of feta with black olives, olive oil and pine kernels in brined vine leaves to bake, but this simple Greek peasant pie is worth the little extra effort. Serve at room temperature as part of a summer buffet, with a rich tomato sauce on the side (see page 184). – Sonia

1 bunch spring onions (about 8), very finely chopped

²/₃ cup (160 ml) fresh mint leaves, chopped

²/₃ cup (160 ml) fresh dill, finely chopped

²/₃ cup (125 g) coarse maize meal, polenta or rice

¼ cup (60 ml) pine kernels, toasted

4 cups (1 litre) thick Greek yoghurt

salt and pepper

20–24 vine leaves in brine, drained and soaked in warm water for 15 minutes before patting dry

olive oil for drizzling

1. Preheat the oven to 170 °C.
2. Spray a 25 cm springform cake tin very well with non-stick cooking spray on the sides and bottom.
3. Stir together the spring onions, herbs, maize meal, polenta or rice, pine kernels and yoghurt until very well blended. Season well.
4. Line the cake tin with half the vine leaves, smooth side down. Spoon in the filling and cover with the remaining vine leaves. Neatly tuck in the sides.
5. Drizzle the whole pie with a little olive oil, cover with heavy foil and bake in the centre of the oven for 1–1¼ hours. The pie should feel firm under your fingers when lightly prodded.
6. Remove and allow to cool under foil for 30 minutes before serving in wedges with a rich tomato sauce alongside.

Serves 8

PESTO, GRUYÈRE AND MUSTARD CAULIFLOWER CHEESE

A humble favourite, given a twist with some store-cupboard basics, becomes a royal treat. Serve with a crunchy garden salad and lots of crusty bread. Use half cauliflower, half broccoli or just broccoli if you like.

1 large cauliflower, trimmed and broken into large florets

1½ cups (375 ml) warm milk

2 T (30 ml) butter

2 T (30 ml) cake flour

salt and pepper

1 t (5 ml) mild mustard

½ cup (125 ml) grated Gruyère or other strong cheese

¼ cup (60 ml) pesto

handful of dried breadcrumbs

1. Preheat the oven to 180 °C.
2. Bring a pot of salted water to the boil and cook the cauliflower for about 4 minutes until just tender. Drain and put in an ovenproof dish.
3. Make the cheese sauce by bringing the milk and butter to the boil in a saucepan. Whisk in the flour until smooth. Turn down the heat to low and cook gently for about 10 minutes, stirring occasionally to prevent scorching.
4. Season and stir in the mustard and cheese.
5. Pour over the cauliflower and dot with pesto. Sprinkle over the breadcrumbs and bake for about 45 minutes, until golden brown and crusty on top.

Serves 4

JADE'S LEMON AND BASIL RISOTTO

I used to cram all the flavours I could find into one dish; nowadays I prefer to let simple flavours like basil and lemon speak for themselves. - Jade

4 cups (1 litre) vegetable stock
350 ml dry white wine
juice and zest of 4 lemons, about
    ¼ cup (60 ml)
1 onion, peeled and chopped
4 stalks from inner part of celery, very
    finely chopped along with the leaves
3 T (45 ml) butter
1 t (5 ml) crushed fresh garlic
2 cups (500 ml) risotto rice, unrinsed
handful of fresh basil, chopped
½ cup (125 ml) grated Parmesan
½ cup (125 ml) mascarpone
salt and freshly ground black pepper

1. Bring the stock, wine and lemon juice to the boil in a small saucepan, then turn down the heat and keep warm while you cook the risotto.
2. Cook the onion and chopped celery stalks in the butter in a large saucepan over medium heat until soft.
3. Add the garlic and celery leaves and cook for a further 2 minutes.
4. Add the risotto rice, turn up the heat and cook while vigorously stirring clockwise for 2–3 minutes, until the rice makes a clicking sound against the sides of the pan.
5. Add a ladleful, about ¾ cup (180 ml), of the pre-prepared stock to the rice, and let it cook stirring clockwise all the while. When all the liquid is absorbed, follow with another ladleful and so on, until all the stock has been used.
6. After 20–25 minutes, the risotto should be a little soupy and the rice cooked, while still retaining a little texture, called 'al dente'. It should NOT be mushy.
7. Briskly stir the basil into the risotto along with the lemon zest, Parmesan and mascarpone. Season liberally with salt and fresh ground black pepper and serve immediately.

Serves 4

Oven-baked cheesy mushroom risotto

6 spring onions, finely chopped
2 t (10 ml) crushed fresh garlic
6 T (90 ml) butter
35 g dried porcini mushrooms, soaked in
    enough warm water to cover
350 g mixed mushrooms (field,
    portabellini, buttons or oyster)
1 t (5 ml) dried thyme or 5 sprigs
    fresh thyme
1½ cups (375 ml) risotto rice, like
    arborio or carnaroli
6 T (90 ml) dry white wine
1 cup (250 ml) hot vegetable or
    mushroom stock
¼ t (1 ml) grated nutmeg
salt and pepper
¼ cup (60 ml) grated Parmesan
200 g very ripe Camembert or
    Brie, crumbled

1. Preheat the oven to 160 °C.
2. Cook the spring onion and garlic in the butter in a large saucepan until soft and aromatic.
3. Drain the soaked porcini, squeeze dry and chop along with the rest of the mushrooms.
4. Add the mushrooms to the saucepan and cook until all the moisture has evaporated.
5. Add the remaining ingredients, excluding the cheeses. Stir well, season and decant to a large ovenproof dish.
6. Bake in the centre of the oven for 20–25 minutes.
7. Sprinkle over the cheeses and continue to bake until firm, golden brown and crusty.

Serves 4

Roast butternut, barley, rocket and orange festive salad

1 kg peeled butternut chunks
1 T (15 ml) olive oil
1 T (15 ml) balsamic vinegar
1 t (5 ml) smoked paprika
salt and pepper
¾ cup (180 ml) pearl barley, rinsed and
    then cooked in 3 cups (750 ml)
    salted water until just tender
grated zest and juice of 1 orange and
    1 lemon
1 t (5 ml) Dijon or mild mustard
1 t (5 ml) honey
2 T (30 ml) red wine vinegar
¼ cup (60 ml) olive oil
handful each of fresh mint, basil, baby
    spinach and rocket
1 small red onion, peeled and very
    thinly sliced

1. Preheat the oven to 200 °C.
2. Cut the butternut into smaller chunks, drizzle with the 1 T (15 ml) olive oil and the balsamic vinegar, and season with the paprika, salt and pepper. Roast for 25 minutes until browned and tender.
3. Cook the barley for about 25 minutes until tender. Drain.
4. Whisk together the orange and lemon juices and zest, mustard, honey, vinegar, salt and pepper. Add the olive oil and whisk to form an emulsion.
5. Arrange the greens on a platter and spoon over the barley and butternut. Scatter over the sliced red onion, drizzle with the dressing and serve.

Serve 4-6

Basil-stuffed polenta squares
with broccoli and four cheeses

6 cups (1.5 litres) vegetable stock or
    water (add 1 t (5 ml) salt to water)
2 cups (500 ml) instant polenta
1/4 cup (60 g) butter
1 cup (250 ml) grated Parmesan
salt and pepper
2 large handfuls (about 80 g) of fresh
    basil leaves, washed and spun dry
4 cups (400 g) grated mozzarella
olive oil for frying
1/2 cup (125 ml) mascarpone
1/2 cup (125 ml) crumbled creamy
    blue cheese
1 large head broccoli, broken into florets
    and steamed

1. Prepare a 20 x 20 cm roasting tin by rubbing with oil and lining with a square of baking paper.
2. Bring the vegetable stock or salted water to the boil in a pot. Stir in the polenta, working fast so there are no lumps. Cook while stirring for 3–4 minutes before removing from the heat.
3. Stir in the butter, Parmesan, salt and pepper and spread half the polenta over the bottom of the prepared tin.
4. Tear the basil leaves with your hands and use to cover the polenta. Sprinkle over the mozzarella and cover with the remaining polenta, making sure to spread right into the corners. Leave to stand for 45 minutes to set.
5. Cut squares from the stuffed polenta and fry on both sides in shallow hot oil until crisp and golden brown.
6. Mix the mascarpone with the crumbled blue cheese.
7. Top each square of fried polenta with some steamed broccoli and blue cheese cream. Flash under a hot grill to melt the cheese if you like.

Serves 4

Mushroom toad in the hole with miso gravy

4 large field mushrooms, quartered, or
    16 medium brown mushrooms
salt and black pepper
2 large eggs
1 cup (250 ml) cake flour
1 t (5 ml) baking powder
1/2 t (2.5 ml) salt
1 1/2 cups (375 ml) dairy or soy milk
8 cherry tomatoes, halved
4–5 sprigs fresh thyme

1. Preheat the oven to 200 °C.
2. Place the mushrooms in a 25 x 12 cm roasting tin, season and roast for 15 minutes until tender.
3. Meanwhile, whisk together the eggs, flour, baking powder, salt, some black pepper and the milk. Leave to stand.
4. Once the mushrooms are cooked, scatter the tomato halves and thyme around them. Quickly pour all the batter into the sizzling-hot tin over the mushrooms and return to the oven.
5. Bake for 20 minutes until the batter is puffed up and golden.
6. Serve smothered in miso gravy (see page 178).

Serves 4

AUBERGINE, RED LENTIL AND TOMATO CURRY

If you can find canned cherry tomatoes, they'd be ideal for this recipe.
Serve with millet or quinoa for a high-protein, low-fat meal.

3 T (45 ml) sunflower oil

1 large aubergine (eggplant), rinsed and
    chopped into chunks

1 medium onion, peeled and chopped

2 t (10 ml) crushed fresh garlic

1 t (5 ml) grated fresh ginger

1 t (5 ml) ground cumin

1 t (5 ml) ground fenugreek

¼–½ t (1–2.5 ml) cayenne pepper

½ cup (125 ml) red lentils, thoroughly
    rinsed under running water

1 cup (250 ml) water

1 x 410 g can whole peeled or
    cherry tomatoes

2 T (30 ml) tomato concentrate

10 curry leaves

chopped fresh coriander leaves,
    poppadoms and plain yoghurt
    to serve

1. Heat 2 T (30 ml) of the oil in a large saucepan and cook the aubergine and onion for about 7 minutes until softened. Remove from the pan with a slotted spoon.
2. Add the remaining oil to the pan, along with the garlic, ginger and spices and cook for 3 minutes while stirring.
3. Add the lentils and water and simmer until the lentils have softened.
4. Add the aubergine and onion, canned tomatoes, tomato concentrate and curry leaves and simmer for 5–10 minutes.
5. Serve on a mound of hot millet or quinoa with chopped fresh coriander, poppadoms and yoghurt.

Serves 4

GINGERED SWEET POTATO SOUP WITH SALTED PEANUTS

This is my own unusual but captivating combination. - Jade

1 onion, peeled and chopped

4 leeks, white part only, rinsed
    and chopped

1 T (15 ml) finely grated fresh ginger

1 red chilli, finely chopped

2 t (10 ml) crushed fresh garlic

2 T (30 ml) olive oil

500 g sweet potatoes, peeled and cubed

4 cups (1 litre) vegetable stock

1 x 400 ml can low-fat coconut milk

salt and pepper

1 cup (250 ml) raw shelled peanuts

1 t (5 ml) sea-salt flakes

handful of fresh coriander, chopped

1. Cook the onion, leeks, ginger, chilli and garlic in the olive oil in a large pot until softened and golden brown.
2. Add the sweet potatoes, stock and coconut milk, season and simmer for about 20 minutes until the potato is completely soft.
3. Pan-roast the peanuts until golden brown and aromatic, season liberally with sea-salt and set aside.
4. Liquidise the soup with the coriander and serve with a garnish of salted peanuts.

Serves 4

SAVOURY PANCAKES BAKED WITH SPINACH, CREAM AND GRUYÈRE

12 pancakes (see page 173)
300 g baby spinach or chard, rinsed,
    dried, stalks removed and chopped
¼ cup (60 ml) butter
salt and pepper
200 g mushrooms, thinly sliced
¾ cup (180 ml) grated Gruyère
    or Parmesan
1½ cups (375 ml) pouring cream

1. First make the pancakes and keep warm in a warming drawer.
2. Preheat the oven to 200 °C and grease an ovenproof dish.
3. Cook the spinach or chard in half the butter in a pot over high heat until just wilted. Season and squeeze out all excess liquid with the back of a spoon. Chop finely.
4. Cook the mushrooms in the remaining butter in a frying pan until all liquid has evaporated.
5. Stir the mushrooms into the cooked spinach, add the grated cheese and season well.
6. Divide the filling between the pancakes, roll up and place in the greased dish. Pour over the cream, season and bake in the centre of the oven for 25–30 minutes until golden brown.

Serves 4

HOMEMADE BAKED BEANS WITH ROAST TOMATOES AND CHILLI—CHEESE CORNBREAD CRUST

Homemade baked beans are a revelation - they are so much tastier than the canned variety. Start the day before you want to cook the beans, to give them a good overnight soak.

400 g small dried white beans
1 sprig fresh thyme
2 bay leaves
½ onion
2 medium onions, peeled and
    finely chopped
3 T (45 ml) butter
1 t (5 ml) sweet paprika
2 t (10 ml) mustard powder
2 T (30 ml) tomato purée
1 cup (250 ml) vegetable stock
6 T (90 ml) sweet molasses (high test)
    or maple syrup
salt and pepper
6 large ripe Rosa tomatoes, halved
1 T (15 ml) olive oil

CORNBREAD TOPPING

1 cup (250 ml) cake flour
½ t (2.5 ml) salt
2 t (10 ml) baking powder
1 t (5 ml) bicarbonate of soda
1 small green chilli, finely chopped
¼ cup (60 ml) grated Parmesan
2 T (30 ml) chopped chives
1 cup (250 ml) yellow polenta
1 cup (250 ml) Bulgarian yoghurt
    or buttermilk
1 large egg
2 T (30 ml) olive oil

1. Soak the beans in plenty of water for at least 8 hours, preferably overnight.
2. When ready to start, drain the beans, cover with water in a saucepan, add the thyme, bay leaves and onion half and bring to the boil.
3. Turn down the heat to medium and simmer for about 45 minutes until the beans are tender. Drain and discard the seasonings.
4. Preheat the oven to 150 °C.
5. Cook the chopped onions in the butter in a large saucepan until soft and translucent, stir in the paprika and mustard powder, and cook for a further 1 minute.
6. Add the cooked, drained beans, tomato purée, stock and molasses or maple syrup. Bring to the boil and season. Pour into an ovenproof dish, cover tightly with two layers of heavy-duty foil and bake for 2 hours until the liquid is thickened into sauce and the beans are very tender.
7. Meanwhile, roast the halved tomatoes on a baking tray in the same oven, drizzled with the olive oil and seasoned with some salt and pepper, until tender. Set aside.
8. To make the cornbread topping, simply stir all the ingredients together into a batter and set aside.
9. When the beans are done, lay the tomatoes on top and spoon over the cornbread batter, making sure to spread it right into the corners.
10. Raise the oven temperature to 180 °C and bake for 45 minutes until a toothpick inserted into the cornbread comes out clean.

COOK'S TIP: The cornbread can be baked on its own with the baked beans and tomato on the side as a light savoury supper served with a tangy salad.

Serves 4

RED WINE, MUSHROOM AND ONION PUFF PASTRY PIE

This rich and hearty pie will fill the house with delectable aromas while cooking. Making individual pot pies is a nice touch for a dinner party. Or leave out the pastry and simply serve the mushroom sauce on rice, mash or pasta with grated Parmesan.

12 whole baby onions, soaked in boiling water for 20 minutes and peeled
2 T (30 ml) olive oil
2 leeks, rinsed and finely sliced
2 stalks celery, chopped
2 medium carrots, peeled and thickly sliced
250 g whole portabellini or button mushrooms
2 t (10 ml) chopped fresh rosemary (strip leaves off woody stalk first)
1 T (15 ml) chopped fresh thyme
1 cup (250 ml) red wine
2½ cups (625 ml) vegetable stock
1 T (15 ml) tomato concentrate
2 medium organic potatoes, peeled and chopped into small chunks
salt and pepper
1 x 400 g roll frozen puff pastry, thawed in fridge overnight
1 egg, beaten

1. Trim the roots off the whole baby onions and cook in the olive oil in a pot with the leeks, celery and carrots over medium heat for about 20 minutes until the vegetables begin to caramelise. Stir frequently to prevent scorching.
2. Add the mushrooms and herbs and cook for a further 10 minutes before adding the red wine, stock, tomato concentrate and potato chunks. Put on the lid and simmer over medium heat for 20–25 minutes until the sauce has thickened and all the vegetables are tender but still holding their shape. Stir well and season to taste.
3. Fill 4–6 pot pie dishes or 1 large pie dish three-quarters full with the mushroom stew and allow to cool completely. In the meantime, preheat the oven to 200 ºC.
4. Cut circles 1 cm wider than the diameter of the pie dishes from the pastry and use to cover the pies, crimping the edges.
5. Cut one or two vents in the pastry lids for steam to escape, and brush with a little beaten egg to ensure a golden brown colour.
6. Bake in the centre of the oven for 20 minutes or until the pastry looks puffy and golden brown all over. Serve piping hot.

Serves 4-6

GRILLED AUBERGINE WEDGES WITH MOROCCAN RICE AND TOMATO JAM

This is a delectable meal, served hot or cold.

4 medium aubergines (eggplants), rinsed
    and cut lengthways into wedges
3 T (45 ml) olive oil
1 t (5 ml) ground cumin
1 t (5 ml) smoked paprika
salt and pepper
2 T (30 ml) each of chopped fresh mint
    and coriander leaves
2 t (10 ml) sumac

MOROCCAN RICE

2 cups (400 g) basmati rice, rinsed in
    a sieve under running water until
    the water runs clear
3 T (45 ml) olive oil
1 red onion, peeled and finely chopped
1 t (5 ml) each of ground cinnamon
    and cumin
2 bay leaves
3 cups (750 ml) vegetable stock
¼ cup (60 ml) lemon or lime juice

SPICED YOGHURT

1 cup (250 ml) Greek yoghurt
1 T (15 ml) dried dill
1 T (15 ml) crushed fresh garlic
2 T (30 ml) pine kernels, toasted

TOMATO JAM

1 small onion, peeled and very
    finely chopped
1 T (15 ml) olive oil
1 kg ripe Rosa tomatoes,
    coarsely chopped
1 t (5 ml) ground cinnamon
1 t (5 ml) red wine vinegar
¼ cup (60 ml) chopped fresh coriander
1 T (15 ml) honey

1. Preheat the oven to 200 °C. Place the aubergine wedges on a baking tray and brush with olive oil. Season with cumin, paprika, salt, pepper, mint, coriander and sumac and roast in the oven for 15–20 minutes until just tender. Remove and keep warm.
2. Meanwhile, cook the rice in a saucepan with the olive oil, onion, spices, stock and lemon or lime juice for about 20 minutes until tender.
3. Mix the yoghurt with the dill, garlic and pine kernels and chill in the fridge.
4. To make the jam, soften the onion in the olive oil in a saucepan until translucent. Add the tomatoes and cook on high heat for 10 minutes. Turn down the heat, add the cinnamon, vinegar and coriander and cook gently for a further 35–40 minutes until thick. Stir in the honey and cook for another 10 minutes until the oil separates out of the jam. Bottle in a sterilised glass jar and refrigerate. This will keep in the fridge for 3 weeks.
5. Serve the aubergine wedges on the rice with dollops of spiced yoghurt and tomato jam.

Serves 4

Braai ideas

- Kebabs of sweetcorn, mushrooms, red pepper, halloumi and green herb marinade.
- Cubed ciabatta and mushroom kebabs with rosemary, thyme, garlic and olive oil marinade.
- Aubergine rolled around slices of sweet pepper with smoky BBQ marinade, grilled until softened.
- Kebabs of halloumi, pineapple, green pepper and butternut with chilli—lime coriander marinade.
- Baked onions stuffed with grated Gruyère, breadcrumbs, onions and walnuts — parboil the onions, stuff and wrap in foil, and bake for 1½ hours until very tender.
- Stir some crushed garlic into mascarpone and sour cream, season and serve with char-grilled baby potatoes threaded on woody rosemary stems.

Brandied figs and mascarpone

An easy, boozy pud for those lazy fire-side evenings.

16 organic dried figs
3 cups (750 ml) brandy
2 T (30 ml) honey
½ cup (125 ml) fresh naartjie or
    orange juice
250 g mascarpone
3 T (45 ml) soft brown sugar
3 tots (75 ml) of Drambuie or Cointreau
    (orange liqueur) or brandy
grated zest of 1 orange

1. Soak the figs in the 3 cups of brandy, honey and naartjie or orange juice overnight or for up to 1 week.
2. To serve, beat the mascarpone with the sugar, Drambuie or Cointreau or brandy. Lift the soaked figs out of the brandy, divide between four plates and spoon over the mascarpone. Garnish with orange zest.

Serves 4

RHUBARB AND STRAWBERRY CRUMBLE

Lovely rosy-hued rhubarb is one of my favourite fruits and this is one of the simplest, yet most delicious, ways of preparing it. - Sonia

3 bunches rhubarb, leaves
    discarded, rinsed and stems
    cut into 4 cm chunks
⅓ cup (80 g) white sugar
juice and grated zest of 1 large orange
200 g strawberries, hulled and halved, or
    left whole if small
½ t (2.5 ml) ground ginger
1½ cups (375 ml) cake flour
90 g brown caramel sugar
125 g cold unsalted butter, diced small

1. Preheat the oven to 180 °C.
2. Cover the rhubarb chunks with the white sugar, orange zest and juice and just enough water to cover in a saucepan. Simmer gently until tender and spoon into a baking dish, juice and all.
3. Scatter over the strawberries.
4. Rub together the dry ingredients and butter until it resembles coarse breadcrumbs, and scatter over the rhubarb and strawberries.
5. Bake in the centre of the oven for 30 minutes. Serve hot or cold with lashings of thick cream or custard.

Serves 6-8

ALMOND CROISSANT BREAD PUDDING WITH CUSTARD

Ever wondered what to do with day-old croissants? Make bread pudding, of course! Almond, cinnamon or chocolate croissants come with built-in flavouring.

2 large eggs
3 T (45 ml) castor sugar
1 vanilla pod, split lengthways and seeds
    scraped out
2 cups (500 ml) dairy, soy or rice milk
5 cm stick cinnamon or
    ½ t (2.5 ml) ground
¼ t (1 ml) grated nutmeg
2 T (30 ml) unsalted butter
4–6 stale croissants
¼ cup (60 ml) seedless raisins
    or sultanas

1. Whisk the eggs, castor sugar and vanilla seeds for 30 seconds in a medium Pyrex bowl.
2. Bring the milk to the boil with the vanilla pod, cinnamon and nutmeg in a saucepan. As soon as it begins to boil, remove from the heat and leave to steep and cool down for 30 minutes.
3. Once completely cool, strain the milk, discarding the vanilla pod and cinnamon stick if used, and pour over the beaten eggs. (The vanilla pod can be rinsed, dried and used again.) Whisk the milk and eggs together.
4. Butter the inside of an ovenproof dish (about 22 x 28 x 6 cm deep) well and tear the croissants into chunks into the dish.
5. Scatter over the raisins or sultanas and then pour over the custard. Leave to steep for at least 1 hour.
6. Preheat the oven to 180 °C.
7. Bake the croissant pudding in the middle of the oven for 40 minutes, until the custard is set and the pudding is puffed up and golden brown. Serve with cream or custard.

Serves 4-6

WHITE CHOCOLATE AND COCONUT PANNA COTTA WITH POMEGRANATE JELLY

This has been adapted from a recipe by Donna Hay.

POMEGRANATE JELLY

2 cups (500 ml) pure pomegranate juice
2 T (30 ml) castor sugar
1 cup (250 ml) pomegranate rubies, plus
    extra to garnish
2 t (10 ml) vegetarian gelling agent such
    as Gelozone or agar-agar
2 T (30 ml) water

PANNA COTTA

4 cups (1 litre) low-fat coconut milk
1 T (15 ml) vegetarian gelling agent such
    as Gelozone or agar-agar
½ cup (125 ml) castor sugar
1 vanilla pod
100 g white chocolate, broken into pieces,
    plus extra to garnish

1. Lightly spray eight 1 cup (250 ml) ramekins with non-stick cooking spray and set aside until needed.
2. First make the jelly by warming the pomegranate juice with the castor sugar in a saucepan over medium heat until the sugar has dissolved. Stir in the pomegranate rubies.
3. Stir the gelling agent into the water and leave to stand until dissolved, then mix into the pomegranate mixture and divide evenly between the ramekins. Chill for 1 hour until firmly set.
4. Once the jelly has set, make the panna cotta. Pour ¼ cup (60 ml) of the coconut milk over the gelling agent and leave to dissolve.
5. Meanwhile, heat the rest of the milk with the castor sugar and vanilla pod in a saucepan to boiling point.
6. Remove from the heat and remove the vanilla pod. Add the chocolate pieces and whisk in the gelling agent. Leave to stand until the chocolate has melted, then whisk until smooth.
7. Pour some of the panna cotta into each ramekin, nearly to the top. Stand the filled ramekins on a tray and refrigerate for at least 6 hours until set.
8. When ready to serve, briefly dip the bottoms of the ramekins in a bowl of hot water to loosen the jelly, then unmould onto serving plates. Garnish with pomegranate rubies and shaved white chocolate.

Serves 8

Greek walnut shortbread

Bake

BREADS, CAKES, COOKIES, TARTS AND TREATS

BAKING TIPS

Baking successfully is an immensely satisfying enterprise; it's also healthier and cheaper than store-bought goodies. To maximise your chances of success, adhere to a few simple guidelines:

- Use fresh ingredients. Check sell-by dates and discard stale flour, nuts, baking powder, etc.
- Weight measurements vary considerably for dry ingredients, such as nuts, sugar, flour, etc. Invest in a small digital scale and eliminate the guesswork. As baking is an exact science the dry ingredients in this chapter are measured in grams.
- Have your oven thermostat checked annually and set to the correct temperature.
- Humidity and altitude affect results: make the necessary allowances.

ROSEMARY FLATBREAD WITH APPLE AND SPICE

This is child's play to make. My children love to make it with me. - Sonia

1 x 10 g sachet instant dried yeast
450 g organic white cake flour
¼ cup (60 ml) skim milk powder
1 t (5 ml) salt
2 T (30 ml) very finely chopped fresh
    rosemary leaves
½ t (2.5 ml) ground cumin
2 T (30 ml) olive oil, plus extra
    for brushing
1 cup (250 ml) lukewarm water
1 t (5 ml) honey
¼ cup (60 ml) chopped dried apple
1 T (15 ml) whole fresh rosemary leaves
2 t (10 ml) cumin seeds

1. Stir together the yeast, flour, milk powder, salt, chopped rosemary and cumin until the rosemary is evenly dispersed.
2. In a separate large warmed bowl, stir together the olive oil, water and honey until the honey dissolves.
3. Gradually add the flour, stirring with a wooden spoon to form a soft sticky dough – you may not need all the flour.
4. Turn out the dough onto a lightly floured surface, scatter over the apple and knead for 8–10 minutes until the dough becomes puffy, elastic and warm under your hands. Alternatively, put the dough in your blender with a dough-hook and knead on 3 for 10 minutes. The dough is ready for first rising when it stretches when you pull at it and doesn't break. Another way of checking whether it has been kneaded enough is forming it into a ball and prodding it with a finger – if the indent made slowly rises out again, it's ready for the first rise. (Don't overknead either!)
5. Place the dough in a lightly oiled, warm bowl, roll to cover with a thin film of oil, then cover the bowl with clingfilm and a kitchen towel and leave in a draught-free place to rise until doubled in size: 30–60 minutes depending on the ambient temperature.
6. Preheat the oven to 200 °C. Oil two baking trays.
7. Punch back the dough and knead lightly for 2 minutes.
8. Form into four balls and press each between your palms to 1.5 cm thickness. Place on the baking trays, cover lightly with clingfilm and leave to rise for a further 30 minutes until doubled in size.
9. Brush the flatbreads with extra olive oil, scatter over the rosemary leaves and cumin seeds and bake for 15 minutes until golden brown and the base sounds hollow when tapped.
10. Cool on wire racks and serve warm or at room temperature.

Makes 4

TOMATO AND BASIL FLATBREADS

This bread, known as fougasse, is a classic speciality of Provençal France. This particular recipe is based on one by Ursula Ferrigno in The Family Bread Book. Substitute the cherry tomatoes and basil for other herbs, cheese, roast peppers, roast courgettes, crispy roast potato cubes or pitted olives – anything you fancy. This is wonderful as part of a brunch antipasto platter.

1 T (15 ml) extra-virgin olive oil, plus
    extra for drizzling
290 ml lukewarm water
450 g organic white bread flour
1 t (5 ml) sea-salt flakes, plus extra
    for sprinkling
1 x 10 g sachet instant dried yeast or
    20 g fresh yeast (if using fresh yeast,
    let it sponge with 2 T (30 ml) of the
    warm water)
2 cups (500 ml) cherry tomatoes,
    roughly chopped
handful of fresh basil leaves, torn
    in strips

1. Stir the olive oil into the warm water.
2. Put the flour, salt and instant yeast (if used) in a bowl and stir to mix thoroughly. Make a well in the middle.
3. If using fresh yeast, add the creamed yeast to the dry ingredients now. Gradually add enough of the water and oil mixture, raking the flour into the centre of the well with your fingers, to make a dough. Mix with your hands until the dough pulls away from the sides of the bowl. Keep kneading until your hands come clean.
4. Turn the dough out onto a lightly floured surface and knead for 10 minutes until smooth and elastic, then form into a ball. Put the dough into a warmed, lightly oiled bowl, cover with clingfilm and a kitchen towel and leave in a draught-free place to rise until doubled in size – about 1 hour depending on the ambient temperature.
5. Knock back the dough (punch it to let the air out), turn out on a lightly floured surface and knead for 5 minutes.
6. Divide the dough in half and flatten each piece with the palms of your hands. Scatter the tomatoes and basil evenly over both pieces of dough, then roll them up like sausages.
7. Flatten each sausage and cut in half so you have four even-sized pieces. Use a sharp knife to make four deep diagonal cuts in each loaf. Prise the cuts apart with your fingers to achieve a ladder-like effect.
8. Place the loaves on oiled baking trays and cover with lightly oiled clingfilm. Leave to rise for 1 hour until doubled in size.
9. Preheat the oven to 220 °C.
10. Just before baking, drizzle some olive oil over each loaf, sprinkle over a little salt and bake for 25–30 minutes until golden brown and crusty.

Makes 4

BASIC WHITE BREAD

The secret to baking really good bread at home is straightforward - use top-quality, stoneground bread flour, organic if possible. Instant or fresh yeast can be used, and a really good knead is required to develop the gluten in the dough for a light and airy texture. Use your blender and its dough-hook for easy kneading if your arms don't feel up to it! Nothing beats the smell of homemade bread baking in the oven. Fresh yeast is easily obtained from any supermarket bakery - about 20 g is enough for 750 g flour.

1 x 10 g sachet instant dried yeast or 15 g fresh yeast
700 g unbleached, stoneground strong white bread flour
½ T (7.5 ml) salt
2 T (30 ml) wheatgerm
1 t (5 ml) honey
425 ml tepid water

1. If using instant yeast, mix with the flour, salt and wheatgerm before adding the liquid. If using fresh yeast, dissolve the honey in the warm water and crumble in the yeast. Leave to sponge for about 5 minutes.

2. Put the flour, salt, wheatgerm and instant yeast (if used) in a large, slightly warmed bowl. Make a well in the centre. Dissolve the honey in the water and slowly add this to the dry ingredients, all the while raking flour into the well with your fingers. Keep mixing until the dough forms a sticky ball. Turn out on a lightly floured surface.

3. Work the ball of dough with your hands until your hands come clean – the ball of dough should be firm but not hard. If it feels soft and sticky, add a little extra flour and work into the dough, about 1 T (15 ml) at a time. If the dough feels dry and crumbly, add a little extra water, 1 T (15ml) at a time.

4. Keep kneading with the base of your hand, pushing the dough away from you and pulling it back to form a ball. Do this for 10–15 minutes until the dough starts feeling puffy and warm under your hands. The dough should stretch when it's ready, and not break.

5. Lightly oil a large bowl and rest the ball of dough in it, rubbing a little oil all over the ball as well. Cover with clingfilm and a couple of clean, dry cloths and set aside to rise until the dough has doubled in size – 1–1½ hours or overnight in the refrigerator.

6. Punch down the risen dough and reform into a ball. Knead again for another minute or so, form into a loaf and place on a greased baking tray or in a loaf tin lightly sprayed with non-stick cooking spray. Cover again with clingfilm or slip the entire tray or tin inside a large plastic bag, blowing air in to inflate it slightly and tying it off tightly. Let the dough rise once more, for about 45 minutes to 1 hour, until doubled in size.

7. Preheat the oven to 220 °C.

8. Uncover the loaf, slash the top deeply a few times with a razor or very sharp knife and bake in the centre of the oven for 35–40 minutes until the base sounds hollow when rapped with your knuckles. If it doesn't, return to the oven for another 5 minutes before testing again. Leave to cool completely on a wire rack before slicing.

COOK'S TIPS: You can make bread rolls and breadsticks out of this dough too – form into the desired shapes after the first rising and leave on baking trays to rise under clingfilm. Brush with sweetened milk and sprinkle with poppy or sesame seeds before baking for 25–30 minutes.
Flavour your basic white loaf by adding 1 cup (250 ml) grated strong cheese and 1 T (15 ml) chopped fresh sage or ½ cup (125 ml) chopped sundried tomatoes and ½ cup (125 ml) pitted chopped black olives. Experiment with your own choice of flavours, remembering that less is more!

Makes 1 large loaf

EASY SEED LOAF

Seed loaf is a Cape classic and a typical spoonbread that requires no kneading – the ingredients are stirred together into a soft batter. If you can stir, you can make it! It lasts well, makes gorgeous toast and freezes beautifully for up to a month. Try freezing individual slices that you can pop into the toaster from frozen.

300 g Nutty Wheat flour
280 g stoneground brown bread flour
140 g stoneground white
    bread flour
15 g instant dried yeast
½ T (7.5 ml) salt
1 T (15 ml) each of sesame, poppy,
    sunflower and linseeds, plus extra
    for sprinkling
1 t (5 ml) honey
3 cups (750 ml) warm water (slightly
    warmer than tepid as brown flour
    absorbs a lot of heat)
1 T (15 ml) oil

1. Mix the flours, yeast, salt and seeds in a large bowl.
2. Dissolve the honey in the warm water and add the oil.
3. Pour the wet mixture into the flour and stir very well with a wooden spoon until thoroughly mixed. It should be the consistency of thick porridge.
4. Spoon into two 500 ml-capacity greased loaf tins, sprinkle over the extra seeds and cover with clingfilm and a few clean, dry cloths. Set aside to rise for about 1 hour until doubled in size.
5. Preheat the oven to 200 °C.
6. Once risen, bake the loaves in the centre of the oven for 30 minutes, then turn down the heat to 180 °C without opening the oven door. (This prevents the seeds scorching.)
7. Bake for a further 30 minutes until golden brown and the bases sound hollow when rapped with your knuckles.
8. Turn the loaves out onto a wire rack and leave to cool completely before slicing. Wrap tightly in clingfilm to store, as this will keep the crusts nice and tender.

Makes 2 medium loaves

ADÈLÉ'S CARROT AND WALNUT CAKE

My mom (Jade's grandma) Adèlé loved baking and her carrot cake was legendary. It's rich with spice, imbued with aromatic citrus zest and crowned with a glorious, tangy cream cheese and walnut icing. This recipe is a family heirloom. Since the batter is very dense, it's customary to use a tube cake tin for this, as the tube conducts the heat to the centre of the cake, which would otherwise remain raw while the exterior reached doneness. The cake will keep for several days in an airtight container. - Sonia

375 g unsifted cake flour
2 t (10 ml) baking powder
1 t (5 ml) bicarbonate of soda
1 t (5 ml) ground cinnamon
½ t (2.5 ml) salt
2 T (30 ml) grated lemon zest
2 T (30 ml) grated orange zest
2 T (30 ml) lemon juice
2 T (30 ml) orange juice
250 g butter, softened
225 g light brown sugar
250 g white granulated sugar
4 large eggs
500 g peeled and coarsely grated carrots
125 g coarsely chopped walnuts
155 g sultanas or seedless raisins
    (optional)

CREAM CHEESE ICING

1 x 230 g tub low-fat cream cheese
1 T (15 ml) lemon juice
1 t (5 ml) grated lemon zest
225 g icing sugar, sifted
155 g coarsely chopped walnuts

1. Sift the flour, baking powder, bicarbonate of soda, cinnamon and salt into a large bowl.
2. Mix the citrus zest and juices and set aside.
3. Preheat the oven to 180 °C. Lightly spray a tube cake tin with non-stick cooking spray.
4. Beat the butter and both sugars at high speed in your blender for 4–5 minutes until light and fluffy. Stop beating every now and then to scrape the butter off the sides and bottom to reincorporate into the mixture.
5. Keeping the blender running, add the eggs one by one, making sure each egg is thoroughly incorporated into the batter before adding the next. Keep beating for a further 3 or so minutes until the mixture is light and thick.
6. Turn the blender to low speed and add the flour mixture (in fourths) alternately with the citrus juice (in thirds), beginning and ending with flour. Beat lightly for 1 minute until smooth.
7. Use a metal spoon to fold in the carrots, walnuts and sultanas or raisins if using. Stir lightly to blend very well, dispersing the additions evenly throughout the batter.
8. Spoon the batter into the cake tin and bake in the centre of the oven for about 1 hour, or until a metal skewer inserted in the centre of the cake comes out clean. (Start testing after 50 minutes.) Remove from the oven and cool in the tin on a wire rack for 20 minutes. Then slide a very sharp knife around the edges to loosen the cake. Turn out of the tin onto a wire rack and cool completely.
9. Once the cake is cooled, you may ice it. Beat all the ingredients for the icing except the nuts until very smooth. Spread over the top of the cake, scatter over the chopped walnuts and serve.

Serves 12

Sour cream cheesecake with raspberry glaze

This is the cheesecake of my childhood memories – my mother Adèlé famously made it with a pineapple glaze, although any berry or fruit glaze would work. Served naked with its sour cream topping it's equally glorious. Make it the day before you intend serving it. – Sonia

200 g Tennis biscuits
125 g unsalted butter, melted
3 x 230 g tubs low-fat cream cheese
1 T (15 ml) finely grated lemon zest
1 t (5 ml) vanilla essence
225 g castor sugar
3 large eggs
¾ cup (180 ml) sour cream or
    crème fraîche
¼ cup (60 ml) lemon juice

RASPBERRY GLAZE
500 g frozen raspberries or any other
    berries, thawed
2 T (30 ml) castor sugar
4 t (20 ml) cornflour
3 T (45 ml) raspberry jam

1. Process the biscuits into fine crumbs in a food processor. Add the melted butter through the chute while the motor is running and blend to combine. Press the crust over the base and against the sides of a 24 cm springform cake tin. Refrigerate for 30 minutes to firm it up.
2. Preheat the oven to 180 °C and remove the crust from the fridge.
3. Beat the cream cheese with the lemon zest, vanilla essence and castor sugar in a large bowl until very smooth. Add the eggs one at a time, blend until thoroughly incorporated and then add the sour cream or crème fraîche and lemon juice. Beat until smooth.
4. Pour the filling onto the prepared crust, smooth over and bake in the middle of the oven on a baking tray for about 1½ hours until set. The top should not be browned – cover it with inverted foil if you are worried this might happen.
5. Remove from the oven and cool completely before refrigerating overnight.
6. About 3 hours before serving, make the glaze by draining the thawed berries, reserving any juice. Add sufficient water to the juice to make 1 cup (250 ml) liquid.
7. Combine the castor sugar, cornflour and juice in a saucepan and stir over medium heat until the sugar has completely dissolved. Bring to the boil and boil for 1 minute.
8. Remove from the heat and cool for 45 seconds before stirring in the berries and jam. Cool completely before pouring over the cheesecake. Return to the fridge for 1 hour to set.

Serves 12

Plum and almond upside-down cake

Fruit and pastry, or cake, make a magical combination. This beauty makes the most of sweetly tart, lushly scented summer plums. Serve with a spiced syrup made from boiling 1 cup sugar, 2 cups water, 3 star anise, a 5 cm stick cinnamon and 3 cardamom pods together until syrupy. Some cold thick cream won't go amiss here either.

50 g unsalted butter
115 g light brown sugar
10 small plums, washed, halved
    and pitted
185 g cold butter, cubed
225 g light brown sugar
3 large eggs
50 g ground almonds
62.5 g cake flour
62.5 g self-raising flour

1. Preheat the oven to 180 °C. Lightly grease a 22 cm springform cake tin and line with lightly greased baking paper.
2. Melt the first amount of butter with the first amount of sugar in a saucepan over medium heat, stirring until the sugar dissolves. Pour into the base of the cake tin.
3. Arrange the plums cut-side down on the melted butter in the tin.
4. Beat the cold butter and second amount of sugar in a large bowl for 4–5 minutes until light and fluffy. Add one egg at a time, making sure each egg is thoroughly incorporated before adding the next.
5. Add the ground almonds and both kinds of flour, and beat for another minute.
6. Spread the batter over the plums in the tin and bake in the centre of the oven for 1 hour, or until a skewer inserted in the middle of the cake comes out clean. (Start testing at 50 minutes.) Remove from the oven and cool for 5 minutes before loosening the sides of the tin. Place a plate upside down on top of the tin and swiftly turn right side up. Carefully remove the base of the tin from the top of the cake. Serve warm or cool.

Serves 10

GLUTEN-FREE CHOCOLATE SPONGE CAKE

This yields a lovely moist cake that will last, un-iced, for several days in an airtight container. If you are wheat sensitive, make sure to use maize cornflour like Maizena, not a wheat-based one.

280 g castor sugar
50 g cocoa powder
110 g cornflour
125 g soy flour
1 t (5 ml) bicarbonate of soda
1 cup (250 ml) soy milk
1 T (15 ml) white vinegar
150 g unsalted butter, melted
1 very ripe banana, well mashed
2 large eggs, beaten
2 T (30 ml) smooth strawberry jam
1 cup (250 ml) non-dairy cream,
   whipped thick

1. Preheat the oven to 180 °C. Spray two 22 cm springform cake tins with non-stick cooking spray and line the bases with baking paper.
2. Sift the dry ingredients into the bowl of your blender.
3. Stir the soy milk, vinegar and butter together and blend with the dry ingredients at low speed for 1 minute.
4. Add the mashed banana, eggs and jam and beat at medium speed for 3 minutes until very smooth.
5. Pour the batter into the cake tins and bake for 30 minutes or until a skewer inserted into the middle of the cakes comes out clean. Remove and cool for 5 minutes before loosening the sides with a spatula. Unclamp the sides and stand the cakes on wire racks to cool completely before sandwiching together with whipped 'cream'.

Serves 8-10

LOW-FAT EGG- AND DAIRY-FREE FRUITCAKE

Yes, you may sin with a clear conscience. This cake contains no eggs or dairy and no added fat or sugar, and is a breeze to make.

225 g pitted dates
300 ml water
175 g wholewheat flour
1 T (15 ml) carob powder
1 T (15 ml) baking powder
1 t (5 ml) mixed spice
grated zest of 1 medium orange
25 g ground almonds
175 g seedless raisins
100 g sultanas
100 g currants
50 g mixed candied peel, finely chopped
¼ cup (60 ml) water
handful of flaked almonds

1. Preheat the oven to 160 °C. Lightly grease a 1 kg loaf tin and line with baking paper.
2. Warm the dates and the first amount of water in a saucepan over medium heat until softened. Remove from the heat and blend the dates with the water to a smooth purée.
3. Mix the remaining ingredients except the almonds with the puréed dates in a large bowl.
4. Spoon into the prepared loaf tin and smooth the top with the back of a moistened spoon.
5. Scatter over the flaked almonds and bake in the middle of the oven for 1½ hours, or until a skewer inserted in the middle of the cake comes out clean. Protect the top of the cake with inverted foil to prevent it over-browning.
6. Remove from the oven and cool for 5 minutes before loosening the sides with a spatula and inverting the cake onto a wire rack. Allow to cool completely before wrapping. It will last up to three months in a cool dry place. You may drizzle a little brandy over it once a week to moisten and flavour it.

Makes 1 loaf

Old-fashioned soetkoekies

Sweetly nostalgic and redolent with heady spices, these cookies were synonymous with Christmas holidays during my childhood. Today my children relish both baking and eating them. The cookies taste better after maturing in the cake tin for a week or so since they are quite hard when freshly baked. They make the perfect midnight snack with a glass of ice-cold milk. - Sonia

350 g cold unsalted butter
180 g treacle sugar
450 g cake flour
4 t (20 ml) ground ginger
4 t (20 ml) ground cinnamon
2 t (10 ml) ground cloves
2 t (10 ml) allspice
grated zest of 1 medium orange

1. Beat the butter and sugar in a mixer at medium speed for about 4 minutes until fluffy and light.
2. Mix the flour with the spices and grated zest and add to the creamed butter. Beat at medium speed for about 3 minutes until thoroughly blended.
3. Remove the dough from the mixer and knead on a lightly floured surface for about 4 minutes. Shape into a ball, wrap tightly in clingfilm and refrigerate for at least 30 minutes. (The dough lasts up to 2 weeks in the fridge.)
4. Preheat the oven to 190 °C. Remove the dough from the fridge 15 minutes before you want to start rolling. Line three baking trays with baking paper.
5. Roll out the dough on a lightly floured surface to about 0.5 cm thick and cut out shapes using cookie cutters. Place on the baking trays and bake for 15 minutes until light golden brown. Remove and cool on wire racks before storing in airtight containers for up to 1 week.

Makes 24-30

CHOC-CHIP, CRANBERRY, COCONUT AND OAT BARS

Use an equal amount of soft dried apricots if you can't find dried cranberries, and use dark or white chocolate chips, or both!

1 T (15 ml) organic honey
115 g firmly packed soft brown sugar
125 g butter
½ t (2.5 ml) ground cinnamon
75 g dried cranberries
¼ cup (60 ml) sunflower seeds
¼ cup (60 ml) desiccated coconut
2 T (30 ml) chocolate chips
200 g rolled oats

1. Preheat the oven to 160 °C. Spray a 20 x 30 cm cake tin with non-stick cooking spray and line the base and sides with two rectangles of baking paper, leaving several centimetres spare above the edges of the tin.
2. Melt the honey, sugar and butter in a saucepan over medium heat and set aside.
3. Mix all the remaining ingredients, pour in the melted butter and stir until well blended.
4. Press evenly into the prepared cake tin and bake in the middle of the oven for 30 minutes until light golden brown. Remove and cool for 3 minutes before cutting into squares. Cool completely before clasping the paper sticking out over the edges and lifting to get the squares out of the tin.

Makes 8-10

GREEK WALNUT SHORTBREAD

Crescent-shaped and heavily dusted with icing sugar, kourabiedes are served during Easter and other festive holidays and are delicious with strong Turkish coffee. You can shape the dough into balls or fingers if you prefer.

250 g unsalted butter
110 g icing sugar, sifted twice, plus extra
    for dusting
1 t (5 ml) vanilla essence
1 large egg yolk
300 g cake flour, sifted
½ t (2.5 ml) baking powder
90 g walnuts, very finely chopped
2 T (30 ml) orange flower water

1. Preheat the oven to 160 °C. Line three baking trays with baking paper.
2. Beat the butter in a large mixing bowl until pale and creamy, then add the icing sugar, vanilla essence and egg yolk. Beat until thoroughly incorporated.
3. Add the flour, baking powder and walnuts and stir very well to combine.
4. Pinch off tablespoonfuls of the dough and roll into little sausage shapes, which you bend into crescents. Place them 3 cm apart on the lined baking trays and bake for 15–20 minutes until light golden brown.
5. Remove from the oven and sprinkle the cookies with orange flower water. Dust with icing sugar while still warm and allow to cool completely. Once cool, dust with more icing sugar — it should literally puff up in little clouds as you bite into the cookies! Store in an airtight container for up to 2 weeks.

Makes 24-26

Oatcakes

These are great with cheese and are a tasty treat for those with wheat intolerance.

175 g medium oatmeal (available at health stores), plus extra for rolling
½ t (2.5 ml) salt
15 g unsalted butter
150 ml boiling water

1. Mix the oatmeal, salt, butter and boiling water in a bowl. Stir until you've got a sticky dough.
2. Let the dough stand for 5 minutes for the oatmeal to absorb the water and expand, which will make the dough pliable.
3. Preheat the oven to 180 °C. Grease two baking trays.
4. Turn out the dough onto a surface lightly dusted with oatmeal and roll out very thinly, about 2 mm. Cut out circles with cookie cutters and lift onto the baking trays with an egglifter. Bake for 15–20 minutes until dry but not browned. Remove and cool to crisp up before storing in an airtight container.

Makes 20-24

Rough puff pastry

Store-bought frozen pastry is a boon when you're busy, but a good homemade rough puff pastry can't be beaten for a hearty pie.

200 g cake flour
¼ t (1 ml) salt
75 g very cold white margarine, diced
75 g very cold unsalted butter, diced
1 t (5 ml) lemon juice
100 ml cold water

1. Stir the flour and salt into a large mixing bowl.
2. Swiftly blend the cold margarine and butter into the flour with a knife, using a cutting motion. Don't break up the lumps.
3. Stir in the lemon juice and cold water and quickly mix to a stiff dough – on no account let the fats warm or melt.
4. Roll out the dough on a lightly floured surface to form a rectangle about 30 x 10 cm. Place it with the longest side running horizontally on the surface in front of you.
5. Fold the top third of the pastry down in a strip towards the middle and the bottom third up. Pinch the edges to close them.
6. Turn the pastry 90 degrees and start rolling into a rectangle as before. Repeat steps 4 and 5 altogether four times, letting the pastry rest for 15 minutes between each repetition of folding and rolling so it doesn't get too warm.
7. Wrap in clingfilm and rest in the fridge at least 30 minutes before using.

Makes about 400 g

DINE'S FOOLPROOF PANCAKE BATTER

There is simply no better pancake recipe than this. I share it with you with kind permission from my friend, Dine van Zyl, writer and author of several cookbooks on traditional South African cooking, or boerekos. - Sonia

125 g cake flour
1 t (5 ml) baking powder
½ t (2.5 ml) salt
2 large eggs
2 cups (500 ml) milk
1 T (15 ml) melted butter
sunflower oil

1. Beat the flour, baking powder, salt, eggs and milk in a food processor or blender for 8 minutes at high speed.
2. Let the batter stand for no less than 30 minutes and up to 1 day in the fridge.
3. Just before cooking, whisk in the melted butter.
4. Pour just enough oil into a medium non-stick frying pan or crêpe pan to coat the bottom. Heat over medium heat until the oil starts to move and then pour out into a heat-proof bowl.
5. Using a ¼ cup (60 ml) measure, pour batter into the pan, swirling the pan around to coat the entire bottom. Cook until small holes appear in the surface, loosen the edges with a spatula and immediately flick the pancake over to cook for about 35 seconds on the other side.
6. Slide out onto a warmed plate and continue until all the batter is used up. Remember to re-oil the pan every fourth pancake or so, wiping away excess oil with absorbent paper towel.

COOK'S TIP: For some reason, the first pancake is usually a flop, which makes the household pets very happy! You'll attain best results by reserving a pan solely for the purpose of making pancakes, since the tiniest scratch on the surface will make the pancakes stick. Practice makes perfect.

Makes 12-18

RICH TOMATO SAUCE

Basics

SELF-SUFFICIENT STORE-CUPBOARD

ORGANIC VEGETABLE BROTH

Commercial stock cubes or granules are often high in salt and laced with additives. Making your own from fresh organic produce is a breeze - and since it freezes well you can make the most of a glut and simmer up some fragrant stock. A word of caution: tired old veggies are meant for the compost heap and not your stockpot. Cruciferous vegetables such as broccoli, cauliflower and cabbage will lend an unpleasant funky taste to your broth and are best avoided.

If you know your vegetables are unsprayed and guaranteed organic, by all means add a handful or two of carrot or potato peelings, leafy tops or stems.

To make a sparklingly clear broth, bring the stock to a fast boil and then turn off the heat completely to let the vegetables sink to the bottom of the pot. Allow to stand for 30 minutes, then turn to a medium heat and simmer gently for an hour before straining and discarding the solids.

4 stalks celery, chopped
2 large leeks, green parts sliced away and
    the remainder washed thoroughly
3 large carrots, peeled and chopped
3 large onions, peeled and chopped
1 whole head garlic, sliced in half across
20 black peppercorns
4 sprigs fresh thyme
4 bay leaves
5 stalks fresh parsley
1 sprig fresh origanum or 1 t (5 ml) dried
1 cup (250 ml) dry white wine or water
2 litres cold water

1. Put all the ingredients in a large pot and bring to a fast boil. Turn off the heat, put on the lid and leave to steep for 30 minutes.
2. Bring back to a simmer and cook gently for 1 hour. Strain through a colander and discard the solids. Reduce in volume to 2 litres and allow to cool completely before freezing for up to 1 month. It will keep in the fridge for up to 1 week.

Makes 2 litres

COOK'S TIP: Reduce the broth rapidly over high heat to make a concentrated liquid to use as a base for a rich sauce. Add chopped dried mushrooms and mushroom stems for a rich mushroom broth, or stir in 2 T (30 ml) tomato concentrate per 3 cups (750 ml) for a tomato broth to use in risottos or pasta dishes. Cook barley, pasta or rice in plenty of broth with some fresh herbs and diced vegetables for simple, nourishing soups when you are feeling poorly.

DUKKAH

Dukkah is healthy, moreish and far less expensive to make than buy. Serve dukkah with bowls of fruity extra-virgin olive oil and chunks of freshly baked bread for dipping: bread first into the oil, then into the dukkah, then into the mouth! Bake your own bread with a recipe from the Bake chapter.

150 g hazelnuts
75 g sesame seeds
75 g coriander seeds
50 g cumin seeds
¼ t (1 ml) dried thyme
¼ t (1 ml) dried marjoram
¼ t (1 ml) dried lemon peel
salt and pepper

1. Roast the hazelnuts on a baking tray at 180 °C until the skins darken. Rub the warm nuts in a clean kitchen towel until the skins come off. Set to one side to cool.
2. Now toast the sesame, coriander and cumin seeds for about 5 minutes until lightly golden brown. Cool completely.
3. Grind all the ingredients together in a food processor until crumbly – it must not be a powder. It will keep in a cool place in an airtight container for about 1 week.

Makes about 350 g

THAI GREEN CURRY PASTE

100 g fresh green chillies
70 g onions or shallots, peeled and very
    finely chopped
1 T (15 ml) crushed fresh garlic
3 T (45 ml) very finely chopped galangal
    or fresh ginger
4 stalks lemongrass, coarse outer hull
    discarded; and very finely chopped
1 T (15 ml) grated lime zest
1 t (5 ml) very finely chopped
    coriander root
2 T (30 ml) ground white pepper
1 T (15 ml) ground coriander
    seeds, toasted
1 T (15 ml) ground cumin seeds, toasted

1. Process all the ingredients together into a smooth paste. Spoon into a Ziploc bag or airtight container and keep in the fridge for up to 1 month.

Makes about 300 ml

HARISSA

225 g fresh red chillies, deseeded and
    coarsely chopped
1–2 T (15–30 ml) crushed fresh garlic
½ T (7.5 ml) ground coriander
1 T (15 ml) ground caraway seeds
3 T (45 ml) chopped fresh coriander
1 T (15 ml) dried mint or 2 T (30 ml)
    chopped fresh
1 T (15 ml) salt
1 T (15 ml) tomato paste
1 t (5 ml) castor sugar
2–3 T (30–45 ml) olive oil, plus extra

1. Process all the ingredients except the olive oil to a smooth paste, then drizzle the oil into the bowl while the blade is running to moisten the harissa.
2. Spoon into sterilised glass jars and drizzle more olive oil on top to seal the surface. Refrigerate for up to 1 month.

Makes about 300 ml

MISO GRAVY

4 t (20 ml) wholewheat flour
2 T (30 ml) olive oil
2 t (10 ml) dark miso
300 ml warm water
2 T (30 ml) light soy sauce or tamari
½ t (2.5 ml) balsamic glaze or to taste
salt if needed

1. To make the miso gravy, brown the flour in the olive oil in a saucepan over mild heat for a few minutes until it smells aromatic and nutty.
2. Dissolve the miso in the warm water and whisk slowly into the flour. Keep stirring until thickened.
3. Simmer gently for 8–10 minutes, then add the soy sauce or tamari and balsamic glaze to taste. Add salt if you find it necessary.

Makes about 1 ½ (375 ml) cups

HOISIN SAUCE

2 T (30 ml) honey or molasses
4 t (20 ml) white or rice vinegar
8 T (120 ml) soy sauce (use dark, light
    or sweet Indonesian, whatever
    your prefer)
¼ cup (60 ml) smooth peanut butter or
    black bean paste (look under Oriental
    products in the shops)
¼ t (1 ml) garlic powder
½ t (2.5 ml) Tabasco or other chilli sauce
½ t (2.5 ml) fine black pepper

1. Stir the honey or molasses into the vinegar until dissolved and then add the remaining ingredients. Stir very well until smooth.
2. Store in an airtight container in the fridge for up to 1 month.

Makes about 1 cup (250 ml)

SWEET AND TANGY BBQ SAUCE

This is great on vegetables such as aubergines, sweet potato slices, courgettes, field mushrooms and corn on the cob.

2 t (10 ml) crushed fresh garlic
1 t (5 ml) sweet paprika
½ t (2.5 ml) salt
¼ cup (60 ml) clear honey
¼ cup (60 ml) orange or apple juice
3 T (45 ml) tomato purée
6 T (90 ml) light soy sauce
¼ cup (60 ml) white wine or cider vinegar

1. Blend all the ingredients together until smooth and pour over vegetables as desired.
2. Marinate for 1 hour to 2 days in the fridge.
3. To prepare, remove the vegetables from the marinade and simmer the remaining sauce until thickened to use as a baste during grilling or roasting.

Makes about 300 ml

CREAMY GREEK SALAD DRESSING

In this dressing the feta is blended into the sauce to add a lovely salty tang. It's perfect drizzled over a bowl of sun-ripened tomatoes, juicy cucumbers, black olives, radishes and red onion.

1–2 t (5–10 ml) crushed fresh garlic
2 T (30 ml) red wine vinegar or
    lemon juice
150 g feta cheese, crumbled
1 cup (250 ml) Bulgarian yoghurt
6 T (90 ml) extra-virgin olive oil
1 t (5 ml) dried origanum
salt and black pepper

1. Blend the garlic, vinegar or lemon juice, feta, yoghurt, olive oil and origanum together until smooth.
2. Adjust the seasoning – it might be salty enough. If it's too thick, add a few tablespoons of water. Keep in an airtight contained in the fridge for up to 1 week.

Makes about 1 ½ cups (375 ml)

ORANGE-HAZELNUT VINAIGRETTE

I love this dressing with a mixture of baby salad leaves, green herbs and some chopped, toasted hazelnuts scattered over. - Sonia

1 t (5 ml) Dijon mustard
pinch of salt and black pepper
1 T (15 ml) sherry vinegar
2 t (10 ml) orange or grapefruit juice
2 T (30 ml) sunflower oil
2 T (30 ml) hazelnut oil
1 T (15 ml) grated orange zest (optional)

1. Whisk the mustard with the salt, pepper, vinegar and juice in a small jug or bowl.
2. Slowly add the oils while whisking so the dressing emulsifies. Add the grated orange zest if using.
3. Store in a clean, dry glass bottle or jar in the fridge for up to 2 weeks. If the dressing separates while standing, just give it a good whisk or shake in the jar to emulsify again.

Makes about 100 ml

GINGER MISO DRESSING

Use mild white miso to make this dressing that pairs very well with steamed green beans or broccoli, and grilled courgettes or aubergines. It's good with eggs, avocado and asparagus too.

2 T (30 ml) mild white miso
¼ cup (60 ml) rice vinegar
1 T (15 ml) mirin (sweet Japanese rice wine) or dry sherry
1 T (15 ml) castor sugar
2 t (10 ml) grated fresh ginger
1 T (15 ml) water
2 t (10 ml) light soy sauce
2 t (10 ml) sesame oil

1. Warm the ingredients together in a saucepan over low heat until the miso and sugar have dissolved.
2. Whisk until smooth and leave to cool completely before straining through a sieve into a jar. It will keep in the fridge for up to 2 weeks.

Makes ½ cup (125 ml)

LOW-FAT CREAMY DRESSING

In America this is known as 'ranch dressing' and is commonly served with crisp lettuces or salads containing avocado, spinach, cheese and nuts. It's perfect for pasta and potato salads. Using non-fat mayonnaise and yoghurt with the buttermilk achieves a creamy texture with precious little fat content.

6 T (90 ml) fresh buttermilk
½ cup (125 ml) fat-free sour cream
¼ cup (60 ml) fat-free plain yoghurt
2 T (30 ml) fat-free or tofu mayonnaise (see page 181)
½ t (2.5 ml) salt
½ t (2.5 ml) ground black pepper
1 T (15 ml) rice or cider vinegar
1 T (15 ml) finely chopped fresh parsley
1 T (15 ml) finely chopped fresh basil
1 T (15 ml) finely chopped chives
1 T (15 ml) finely chopped fresh dill
1–2 t (5–10 ml) crushed fresh garlic
lemon juice

1. Whisk all the ingredients together until very smooth, adding the lemon juice last to taste.
2. Decant into a clean, glass jar with a tight-fitting lid and keep in the fridge for up to 3 days.

Makes about 300 ml

Fat-free tofu mayonnaise

Use silken, not firm, tofu for this vegan version of mayonnaise. Add 1 T (15 ml) olive oil if you don't mind a bit of oil in your diet.

125 g silken plain tofu
6 T (90 ml) lemon juice, or cider or
    balsamic vinegar
1 T (15 ml) Dijon or other mild mustard
½ t (2.5 ml) wasabi powder (optional)

1. Whisk or process all the ingredients together until very smooth and allow to stand for 30 minutes for the flavours to develop. This will keep in an airtight container in the fridge for up to 1 week.

Makes about 1 cup (250 ml)

Hummus

Using canned chickpeas for homemade hummus certainly speeds things up considerably, but once in a while you might like to make an extra effort and soak some organic chickpeas overnight and simmer them slowly until tender. Tahini is sesame paste that can be bought from most good health shops or the health-food section of your supermarket, and lasts almost forever in the fridge.

1 x 410 g can chickpeas, rinsed
    and drained
1 t (5 ml) crushed fresh garlic
3 T (45 ml) tahini
1 t (5 ml) ground cumin
3–4 T (45–60 ml) olive oil, plus extra
    for drizzling
3 T (45 ml) lemon juice
salt and pepper
paprika for sprinkling

1. Process the chickpeas, garlic, tahini, cumin and half the olive oil together until finely chopped. Stop the motor and push the paste down the sides of the bowl with a spatula before continuing.
2. Add the lemon juice, salt and pepper and continue processing until the desired consistency is reached – add 2 T (30 ml) water if you like your hummus very smooth and almost satiny. Sprinkle with some paprika and a drizzle of olive oil to serve.

Makes about 2 ³/4 cups

Basil oil

large handful (about 80 g) of fresh basil
    leaves, stalks removed
1½ cups (375 ml) extra-virgin olive oil

1. To make the basil oil, bring a large pot of water to the boil. Plunge the basil into the boiling water for 30 seconds and remove quickly. Rinse briefly under cold water and pat dry with absorbent paper towel.
2. Blend the basil in a liquidiser with the olive oil until very smooth. Pour into a sterilised screw-top glass jar and refrigerate until needed. It will keep for about 2 weeks.

Makes about 1 ¹/2 cups (375 ml)

RICOTTA

Ricotta is extremely easy to make provided you use a thermometer. Muslin can be tricky to find, so use a clean, lightly rinsed J-cloth instead to line the strainer.

8 cups (2 litres) fresh low-fat cow's or
    goat's milk
4 cups (1 litre) buttermilk

1. Place a large strainer or fine-holed colander in the sink and line with dampened muslin or a rinsed clean J-cloth.
2. Take a large stainless-steel pot (about 6 litre capacity) and gently heat the milk to 90 °C.
3. Remove from the heat and whisk in the buttermilk. Let it stand. After a while the whey will start separating from the curd. After 10–15 minutes, when the curds and whey have completely separated, pour it into the lined strainer and leave to drain for about 1–2 hours.
4. Transfer to an airtight container and refrigerate until needed. Use within 3 days.

Makes about 4 cups (1 litre)

VANIE'S LEMON ATCHAR

Chef Vanie Padayachee kindly shared her recipe for traditional Indian lemon pickle, or atchar, with me. Serve as a condiment with curries or dhal. – Sonia

8 lemons
½ t (2.5 ml) ground turmeric
2 T (30 ml) non-iodised coarse salt
1 cup (250 ml) sunflower or peanut oil,
    plus extra for bottling
2 T (30 ml) pickle masala
5 cloves garlic, crushed
5 curry leaves
3 green chillies, split in half

1. Scrub the whole lemons under warm running water and put them in a pot with enough water to cover. Add the turmeric.
2. Bring to a gentle boil and skim off any scum that forms on the surface. Boil for 10 minutes, then remove from the heat, scoop out the lemons with a slotted spoon and cool slightly.
3. Quarter the lemons, place into a large non-reactive bowl and sprinkle generously with the salt.
4. Warm the oil in a saucepan until tepid and add the pickle masala, garlic, curry leaves and chillies. Pour over the lemon quarters and stir gently to mix.
5. Spoon the lemons into a 1 litre-capacity sterilised glass jar or four smaller 250 ml jars, and fill to 1 cm below the brim with oil. Screw on a sterilised lid(s).
6. Allow to mature in a cool dark place for 2 weeks before using, turning the jar upside down every day. Refrigerate once opened and use within 1 month.

Makes about 4 cups (1 litre)

HOMEMADE YOGHURT

Plain, live culture yoghurt is a versatile ingredient in any cook's kitchen. Add it to stews or curries, or spoon dollops onto your favourite warm bean or lentil salads. Or make iced lassi – an Indian beverage made from thinning plain yoghurt with some iced water before blending with either sweet or savoury flavourings like mango, banana or toasted cumin and fresh mint. It's also a great tonic for sun-frazzled skin. And of course it makes a brilliant breakfast with some organic honey drizzled on top and a pinch of cinnamon sprinkled over, with or without granola. Have a go at this easy recipe. The trick is to keep the culturing yoghurt at a constant temperature of 38 °C, which is why a yoghurt maker or thermos flask works so well.

600 ml fresh or long-life full-cream milk
150 ml fresh live natural yoghurt

1. Bring the milk to the boil in a large stainless-steel saucepan so that it bubbles to the brim of the pan. Let it bubble like that for 2 minutes.
2. Remove from the heat immediately and cool to blood temperature – about 38 °C. You should be able to keep your finger in the milk for 10 seconds without it burning.
3. Now gently stir in the natural yoghurt until it is thoroughly blended.
4. Warm a glass bowl or jar or thermos flask by quickly pouring boiling water into the container and out again. Pour the yoghurt into the container.
5. Leave undisturbed in a draught-free, warm place for 7–10 hours to set, after which it can be transferred to an airtight container and kept in the fridge. The cold stops further development of the bacteria that makes the yoghurt set.

COOK'S TIP: Homemade yoghurt is thinner and not as smooth as the commercial variety. If you'd prefer a thicker, creamier texture, add 1–3 T (15–45 ml) skim milk powder to the milk when you boil it. If your yoghurt tastes overly acidic, it means the temperature at which it incubated was too high, and if it tastes too sweet, the temperature while culturing was too low. Using a wide-mouthed, pre-warmed thermos flask circumvents this problem, but some cooks prefer a commercial yoghurt maker. And remember to keep ¼ cup (60 ml) aside to start your next batch of homemade yoghurt!

Makes 3 cups (750 ml)

LABNEH

These Middle-Eastern delights are commonly made from goat's or ewe's milk, and sold packed in oil in jars. Serve them freshly made, rolled in chopped herbs, black pepper or sesame and poppy seeds, or pack them into a sterilised jar, cover with good olive oil and keep in the refrigerator for up to 1 month. They make a lovely appetiser served with pita breads, olives and other meze. Labneh doesn't have to be rolled into balls; it is also frequently served simply spooned into a dish to be scooped up with chunks of bread.

1 kg live natural yoghurt (look out for
    goat's or ewe's milk if you can find it)
1 T (15 ml) sea salt
1 T (15 ml) ground black pepper
1 T (15 ml) fresh rosemary leaves
5 sprigs fresh thyme
4 fresh bay leaves
2 small dried chillies
3 cloves garlic, lightly crushed
600 ml olive oil

1. Line a colander with a clean J-cloth that has been rinsed in water. Place the colander over a bowl large enough to catch any drips.
2. Mix the yoghurt very well with the salt and pepper and spoon into the colander.
3. Cover and leave overnight in the fridge – between 18 and 24 hours will do.
4. Make the labneh balls by rolling teaspoonfuls between your palms. Put the balls on a clean baking tray lined with clingfilm, cover lightly with more clingfilm and leave in the fridge once more for 8–12 hours. This will firm the balls up and dry out any excess moisture.
5. Layer the balls in a sterilised glass jar with the seasonings, cover with olive oil, seal and keep in the fridge for up to 1 month.
6. Serve your labneh, perhaps by rolling in some finely chopped herbs, black pepper, paprika, seeds or chopped nuts.

Makes about 48

RICH TOMATO SAUCE

1 small onion, peeled and finely minced
1/4 cup (60 ml) olive oil
1–2 t (5–10 ml) crushed fresh garlic
6 large fresh basil leaves, minced or
    1/4 cup (60 ml) minced fresh parsley
    or 2 t (10 ml) minced fresh origanum
2 x 410 g cans chopped peeled tomatoes
3 T (45 ml) water
salt and pepper
sugar if needed

1. Cook the onion in the olive oil in a pot until translucent and soft. Add the garlic and herbs and cook for 30 seconds.
2. Add the tomatoes in their juice and the water. Season well and simmer for 10–15 minutes until thickened. The sauce is ready when a spoon dragged across the base of the pot leaves a trail.
3. Mash the tomatoes with a potato masher and adjust the taste with a little sugar if too tart. Use hot or cold.

Makes about 3 cups (750 ml)

Potato gnocchi

Use gnocchi on the day of making. This recipe does not freeze well. It is important to add the flour when the potato is still warm to ensure the gnocchi does not disintegrate.

800 g potatoes, peeled and cut into
    large chunks
salt and pepper
1 egg
2 T (30 ml) warm milk
1½ cups (375 ml) cake flour
    (or as needed)
pinch of ground nutmeg
2 T (30 ml) chopped fresh herbs
    (rosemary, thyme, chives, etc.)

1. To make the gnocchi, cook the potatoes in a pot of boiling water until tender and drain. Turn off the heat, return the potatoes to the pot and put back on the still-hot stove. Allow to steam until all the moisture has evaporated.
2. Mash the potatoes until very smooth. Beat in the seasoning and egg, stir vigorously and then add the milk and stir until smooth. Add the flour, nutmeg and herbs and blend well.
3. Turn out the dough onto a lightly floured surface and knead with your hands until soft and smooth – if it is sticky, add another tablespoon of flour and knead in very well.
4. Divide the dough into six parts and roll each into a 2 cm-thick cylinder. Roll lightly in flour and refrigerate on a baking tray for 10 minutes. Cut off 2 cm pieces and press each lightly with the tines of a fork.
5. Bring a very large pot of salted water to a rollicking boil and cook 8–10 gnocchi at a time for 3–4 minutes until they float to the top. Scoop out with a slotted spoon into an oiled serving dish, and serve with a sauce of your choice.

Serves 4

Gomasio

This delicious seasoned salt is a standby of macrobiotic cooking and one of my favourite kitchen condiments. The aromatic, nutty warmth adds extra texture and flavour to dishes when you're trying to cut down on sodium. Add ¼ t (1 ml) ground ginger for some zing, or 1 t (5 ml) ground toasted seaweed and use with eggs, noodles, steamed vegetables, brown rice or stir-fries. - Sonia

1 cup (250 ml) sesame seeds
2–3 t (10–15 ml) sea-salt flakes

1. Toast the seeds in a dry frying pan over medium heat until aromatic and lightly browned. They should crumble easily between your fingertips when ready.
2. Add the salt and toast for a further 30 seconds or so. Leave to cool completely.
3. Grind to the desired texture with a mortar and pestle or in a clean coffee/spice grinder — you may leave it fairly coarse to add chewiness to a dish. This will keep for up to 3 months in an airtight container.

Makes about 1 cup (250 ml)

Index

Index **187**

Conversion chart

CONVERSION TABLE	
METRIC	IMPERIAL
Teaspoons	
2 ml	¼ tsp
3 ml	½ tsp
5 ml	1 tsp
10 ml	2 tsp
20 ml	4 tsp
Tablespoons	
15 ml	1 Tbsp
30 ml	2 Tbsp
45 ml	3 Tbsp
Cups	
60 ml	¼ cup
80 ml	⅓ cup
125 ml	½ cup
160 ml	⅔ cup
200 ml	¾ cup
250 ml	1 cup
375 ml	1 ½ cups
500 ml	2 cups
1 litre	4 cups

OVEN TEMPERATURES			
	°C	°F	gas mark
very cool	100	200	¼
very cool	120	250	½
cool	150	300	2
moderate	160	325	3
moderate	180	350	4
moderate hot	190	375	5
hot	200	400	6
hot	220	425	7
very hot	240	475	9